THE AUSTRALIAN
Women's Weekly

FAST

180 recipes in less than 35 minutes

acp books

contents

introduction	6
fast mornings	8
fast lunches	48
fast after school	104
fast afternoons	132
fast weeknights	166
fast weekends	240
fast barbecues	336
glossary	386
index	392
conversion chart	399

We have less time to cook than ever, but, paradoxically, now is the time we need to cook more. We're becoming more dependent on takeaway food, our children are becoming unhealthy and food prices are rising — it's time to go back to the kitchen. *Fast* is a book of good food that you can make from start to finish in 35 minutes or less. There are recipes for your whole day — mornings, lunchtimes, afternoons and after-school snacks, weeknights, weekends and barbecues. Preparing and planning meals ahead, and being organised, saves more time than you can imagine.

Here are some ideas for fast meals

> Lean cuts of meat are expensive but cook quickly and need little preparation. The money you spend on them will be saved in energy costs and time. > Fish fillets cook quickly and, like lean meat, need little or no preparation. > Clean the kitchen as you go – wipe down benches and cutting boards – it makes cooking more efficient and reduces clean-up afterwards. > Don't waste your oven – put a cake, pudding or the vegies in at the same time as the meat. > Prepare tomorrow's meal tonight – marinate meats, soak pulses – planning ahead saves time.

fast
mornings

Italian egg, prosciutto and cheese roll

4 eggs
4 focaccia rolls (440g), split
120g taleggio or fontina cheese, sliced thinly
4 slices prosciutto (60g)
8 large fresh basil leaves
tomato sauce
400g can crushed tomatoes
¼ cup (60ml) red wine vinegar
2 tablespoons brown sugar

1 Make tomato sauce.
2 Preheat grill.
3 Fry eggs in heated oiled medium frying pan until cooked as you like.
4 Spread bottom half of each roll with about 1 tablespoon of the tomato sauce; place on oven tray. Layer cheese and prosciutto on rolls; grill until cheese starts to melt. Top each with 2 basil leaves, an egg and remaining tomato sauce; top with remaining roll half.
tomato sauce Combine undrained tomatoes with remaining ingredients in medium saucepan; bring to the boil. Reduce heat; simmer 15 minutes.

preparation time 10 minutes **cooking time** 20 minutes **serves** 4
nutritional count per serving 20.3g total fat (9g saturated fat);
2245kJ (537 cal); 58.8g carbohydrate; 27.5g protein; 4.1g fibre

Apple, pear and ginger juice

We used a green-skinned apple here, but any variety is suitable for this juice.

1 medium unpeeled apple (150g), cored, cut into wedges
1 medium unpeeled pear (230g), cored, cut into wedges
1cm piece fresh ginger (5g)

1 Push apple, pear and ginger through juice extractor into glass.
2 Serve with ice.

preparation time 5 minutes **makes** 1 cup (250ml)
nutritional count per 250ml 0.3g total fat (0g saturated fat);
823kJ (197 cal); 43.1g carbohydrate; 1g protein; 0.2g fibre

Herb omelette with sautéed mushrooms

2 tablespoons finely chopped fresh flat-leaf parsley
2 tablespoons finely chopped fresh chervil
2 tablespoons finely chopped fresh chives
2 tablespoons finely chopped fresh tarragon
50g butter
2 tablespoons olive oil
250g swiss brown mushrooms, halved
½ cup (125ml) water
2 teaspoons finely grated lemon rind
1 tablespoon lemon juice
12 eggs

1 Combine herbs in small bowl.
2 Heat 30g of the butter and 1 tablespoon of the oil in large deep frying pan. Add mushrooms; cook, stirring, 5 minutes. Stir in 2 tablespoons of the water; cook, stirring, until water evaporates and mushrooms are tender. Remove from heat; stir in rind, juice and 2 tablespoons of the herb mixture. Cover to keep warm.
3 Gently whisk eggs and remaining water in a large bowl; whisk in remaining herb mixture.
4 Heat a quarter of the remaining butter and 1 teaspoon of the remaining oil in medium frying pan. When butter mixture bubbles, pour a quarter of the egg mixture into pan; cook over medium heat, tilting pan, until egg is almost set. Tilt pan backwards; fold omelette in half. Cook 30 seconds then slide onto serving plate.
5 Repeat step 4, wiping out pan before each addition to make a total of four omelettes. Serve omelettes topped with sautéed mushrooms.

preparation time 10 minutes **cooking time** 20 minutes **serves** 4
nutritional count per serving 35.3g total fat (12.9g saturated fat);
1714kJ (410 cal); 1g carbohydrate; 22.4g protein; 1.8g fibre

Honeyed ricotta and pears

1 cup (240g) reduced-fat ricotta cheese
2 tablespoons honey
¼ teaspoon finely grated orange rind
¼ teaspoon ground cinnamon
½ large loaf turkish bread (215g), halved
825g can sliced pears, drained, sliced
1 tablespoon honey, extra

1 Preheat grill.
2 Combine cheese, honey, rind and cinnamon in small bowl.
3 Meanwhile, cut bread pieces horizontally; toast cut sides. Spread cheese mixture over toast, top with pear; grill about 2 minutes or until hot. Drizzle with extra honey.

preparation time 5 minutes **cooking time** 5 minutes **serves** 4
nutritional count per serving 7g total fat (3.6g saturated fat); 1397kJ (330 cal); 52.7g carbohydrate; 11.8g protein; 3.9g fibre

Cheesy scrambled eggs with spinach

8 eggs
⅓ cup (80g) reduced-fat spreadable cream cheese
50g baby spinach leaves, chopped coarsely

1 Whisk eggs in medium bowl until combined, then whisk in cheese and spinach.
2 Cook mixture, stirring gently, in heated oiled large frying pan over low heat until almost set. Serve with wholemeal toast, if you like.

preparation time 5 minutes **cooking time** 5 minutes **serves** 4
nutritional count per serving 13.8g total fat (5.4g saturated fat);
790kJ (189 cal); 1g carbohydrate; 15.3g protein; 0.3g fibre

Pineapple and rockmelon frappé

1 small pineapple (900g), chopped coarsely
½ small rockmelon (650g), chopped coarsely
40 ice cubes, crushed
2 tablespoons finely chopped fresh mint

1 Blend or process pineapple and rockmelon, in batches, until smooth; transfer to large jug.
2 Stir in ice and mint; pour into serving glasses. Serve with fresh mint leaves, if you like.

preparation time 10 minutes **makes** 1.5 litres (6 cups)
nutritional count per 250ml 0.2g total fat (0g saturated fat); 213kJ (51 cal); 9.9g carbohydrate; 1.2g protein; 2.5g fibre

Blueberry buttermilk pancakes with bacon

2 cups (300g) self-raising flour
¼ cup (55g) caster sugar
2 eggs
600ml buttermilk
50g butter, melted
1 cup (150g) fresh blueberries
cooking-oil spray
12 thin rindless bacon rashers (360g)
½ cup (125ml) maple syrup

1 Sift flour and sugar into large bowl. Whisk eggs, buttermilk and butter in large jug. Gradually whisk egg mixture into flour mixture until smooth. Stir in berries; pour batter into large jug.
2 Spray heavy-based large frying pan with cooking oil. Pour ¼-cup batter for each pancake into heated pan (you can cook four at a time). Cook pancakes until bubbles appear on the surface; turn, brown other side. Cover to keep warm.
3 Repeat step 2, wiping out pan between batches, to make a total of 18 pancakes.
4 Meanwhile, heat oiled large frying pan; cook bacon until crisp. Drizzle pancakes with syrup, serve with bacon.

preparation time 10 minutes **cooking time** 25 minutes **serves** 6
nutritional count per serving 15.4g total fat (7.7g saturated fat);
2224kJ (532 cal); 71.8g carbohydrate; 24.5g protein; 2.4g fibre

Mixed berry smoothie

2 cups (300g) frozen mixed berries
1¾ cups (480g) vanilla yogurt
2½ cups (625ml) milk
2 tablespoons honey

1 Blend or process ingredients until smooth.
2 Serve sprinkled with extra frozen mixed berries, if you like.

preparation time 5 minutes **makes** 1.5 litres (6 cups)
nutritional count per 250ml 6.8g total fat (4.4g saturated fat);
711kJ (170 cal); 18.2g carbohydrate; 8.2g protein; 1.2g fibre

Ricotta and banana toasts

8 x 1cm-thick slices fruit bread, toasted
1 cup (240g) ricotta cheese
2 large bananas (460g), sliced thickly
2 tablespoons honey

1 Top toasts with cheese and banana; drizzle with honey.

preparation time 5 minutes **serves** 4
nutritional count per serving 10.7g total fat (5g saturated fat);
2199kJ (526 cal); 87.1g carbohydrate; 15.8g protein; 6.6g fibre

Hot mocha

2 cups (500ml) milk
100g dark eating chocolate, chopped coarsely
2 cups (500ml) hot black coffee
1 teaspoon cocoa powder

1 Heat milk in medium saucepan, without boiling.
2 Meanwhile, divide chocolate among four 1¼-cup (310ml) glasses.
3 Stir coffee into milk then pour mixture into glasses. Dust with sifted cocoa powder before serving.

preparation time 5 minutes **cooking time** 5 minutes **serves** 4
nutritional count per 250ml 12.1g total fat (7.5g saturated fat);
920kJ (220 cal); 21.9g carbohydrate; 5.7g protein; 0.4g fibre

Spinach, ham and poached egg

4 eggs
½ large loaf turkish bread (215g), halved
75g baby spinach leaves
150g shaved ham

1 Half-fill large frying pan with water; bring to the boil. Break one egg
into a cup then slide into pan; repeat with remaining eggs. When all
eggs are in pan, allow water to return to the boil. Cover pan, turn off
heat; stand about 4 minutes or until a light film of egg white sets over
yolks. Remove eggs, one at a time, using slotted spoon; place spoon
on absorbent-paper-lined saucer to blot up poaching liquid.
2 Meanwhile, cut bread pieces horizontally; toast cut sides. Top toast
with spinach, ham and eggs.

preparation time 5 minutes **cooking time** 5 minutes **serves** 4
nutritional count per serving 8.4g total fat (2.4g saturated fat);
1062kJ (254 cal); 24.3g carbohydrate; 18.9g protein; 1.9g fibre

Strawberries and cream on brioche

3 eggs
⅓ cup (80ml) milk
1 teaspoon vanilla extract
1 tablespoon caster sugar
6 small brioche (600g), halved
40g unsalted butter
250g strawberries, sliced thinly
⅔ cup (160ml) thickened cream

1 Combine eggs, milk, extract and sugar in large shallow bowl. Submerge brioche in egg mixture.
2 Melt half the butter in large frying pan; cook half the brioche until browned both sides. Remove from pan; cover to keep warm. Repeat with remaining butter and brioche.
3 Serve brioche with strawberries and cream.

preparation time 10 minutes **cooking time** 10 minutes **serves** 6
nutritional count per serving 30.5g total fat (16.5g saturated fat); 2286kJ (547 cal); 53.5g carbohydrate; 13.4g protein; 2.8g fibre

Corn, cheese and carrot omelettes

8 eggs
310g can creamed corn
1 large carrot (180g), grated coarsely
¼ cup finely chopped fresh flat-leaf parsley
½ cup (60g) coarsely grated reduced-fat cheddar cheese

1 Whisk eggs in medium bowl until combined; stir in remaining ingredients.
2 Pour a quarter of the egg mixture into heated oiled small frying pan; cook over medium heat until omelette is set. Fold omelette in half, slide onto plate; cover to keep warm.
3 Repeat step 2, wiping out pan before each addition, to make a total of four omelettes.

preparation time 10 minutes **cooking time** 20 minutes **serves** 4
nutritional count per serving 14.7g total fat (5.6g saturated fat); 1162kJ (278 cal); 15.3g carbohydrate; 19.6g protein; 4g fibre

Roasted cherry tomatoes, fetta, avocado and basil

250g cherry tomatoes, halved
½ large loaf turkish bread (215g), halved
1 medium avocado (250g), sliced thinly
100g piece reduced-fat fetta cheese, crumbled
¼ cup coarsely chopped fresh basil

1 Preheat grill.
2 Grill tomato about 5 minutes or until softened.
3 Meanwhile, cut bread pieces horizontally; toast cut sides. Top toast with avocado, tomato and cheese; grill about 2 minutes or until hot. Serve sprinkled with basil.

preparation time 5 minutes **cooking time** 10 minutes **serves** 4
nutritional count per serving 15.4g total fat (4.7g saturated fat); 1237kJ (296 cal); 25.6g carbohydrate; 12.4g protein; 3.1g fibre

Huevos rancheros

3 chorizo sausages (500g), sliced thickly
8 eggs
½ cup (125ml) cream
20g butter
4 x 15cm flour tortillas
1 cup (120g) coarsely grated cheddar cheese
fresh tomato salsa
2 small tomatoes (180g), chopped finely
½ small red onion (50g), chopped finely
1 tablespoon red wine vinegar
1 tablespoon olive oil
¼ cup coarsely chopped fresh coriander

1 Preheat oven to 160°C/140°C fan-forced.
2 Make fresh tomato salsa.
3 Cook chorizo on heated oiled grill plate (or grill or barbecue) until well browned. Drain on absorbent paper; cover to keep warm.
4 Whisk eggs and cream in medium bowl. Melt butter in medium frying pan; cook egg mixture over low heat, stirring gently, until creamy.
5 Meanwhile, place tortillas on oven tray, sprinkle with cheese; warm in oven until cheese melts.
6 Divide tortillas among serving plates; top with egg, chorizo and salsa.
fresh tomato salsa Combine tomato, onion, vinegar and oil in small bowl; stir in coriander.

preparation time 10 minutes **cooking time** 10 minutes **serves** 4
nutritional count per serving 81.7g total fat (35.8g saturated fat);
4126kJ (987 cal); 16.2g carbohydrate; 48.2g protein; 1.9g fibre

Indian chai

5 cardamom pods, bruised
10 cloves
1 cinnamon stick
1cm piece fresh ginger (5g), sliced thickly
2 teaspoons fennel seeds
1 teaspoon vanilla extract
3 cups (750ml) water
4 darjeeling teabags
2 cups (500ml) milk
⅓ cup (90g) grated palm sugar

1 Combine cardamom, cloves, cinnamon, ginger, fennel, extract and the water in medium saucepan; bring to the boil. Cover; simmer 5 minutes. Remove from heat; stand, covered, 10 minutes.
2 Return spice mixture to the boil, add teabags; remove from heat. Stand 5 minutes.
3 Meanwhile, heat milk in medium saucepan without boiling. Add milk to tea mixture; add sugar, stir until dissolved.

preparation time 5 minutes
cooking time 10 minutes **makes** 1 litre (4 cups)
nutritional count per 250ml 4.9g total fat (3.2g saturated fat); 727kJ (174 cal); 27.9g carbohydrate; 4.3g protein; 0g fibre

Porridge with honeyed coconut and dried fruit

½ cup (25g) flaked coconut
¼ cup (90g) honey
1 ⅓ cups (330ml) low-fat milk
1 cup (250ml) water
1 cup (90g) rolled oats
¼ cup (35g) finely chopped dried pears
2 tablespoons finely chopped sultanas
2 tablespoons finely chopped dried apricots

1 Preheat oven to 180°C/160°C fan-forced. Line shallow medium baking dish with baking paper.
2 Sprinkle coconut into dish; drizzle with 1 tablespoon of the honey. Cook, uncovered, about 5 minutes or until browned lightly. Cool in dish.
3 Meanwhile, stir milk, the water and oats in medium saucepan over medium heat about 10 minutes or until porridge is thick and creamy. Stir in remaining honey and half the dried fruit.
4 Sprinkle porridge with remaining fruit and coconut; serve with warmed milk, if you like.

preparation time 10 minutes **cooking time** 15 minutes **serves** 4
nutritional count per serving 6.2g total fat (4g saturated fat); 1233kJ (295 cal); 47.7g carbohydrate; 7.3g protein; 4.1g fibre

BLT on croissant

We used rindless shortcut bacon here, but you can use trimmed bacon rashers if you prefer.

12 slices rindless shortcut bacon (420g)
4 large croissants (320g)
2 small tomatoes (180g), sliced thinly
8 large butter lettuce leaves
aïoli
½ cup (150g) mayonnaise
1 clove garlic, crushed
1 tablespoon finely chopped fresh flat-leaf parsley

1 Cook bacon in large frying pan until crisp.
2 Preheat grill.
3 Meanwhile, make aïoli.
4 Toast croissants under grill about 30 seconds. Split croissants in half; spread aïoli over one half of each croissant then top with bacon, tomato, lettuce and remaining croissant half.
aïoli Combine ingredients in small bowl.

preparation time 10 minutes **cooking time** 5 minutes **serves** 4
nutritional count per serving 36.8g total fat (13.9g saturated fat); 2592kJ (620 cal); 39.5g carbohydrate; 31.4g protein; 3.8g fibre

Peach and raspberry juice

1 large peach (220g), peeled, chopped coarsely
¼ cup (35g) fresh or frozen raspberries
½ cup (125ml) water

1 Blend or process peach and raspberries until smooth; pour into glass.
2 Stir in the water; serve with ice.

preparation time 5 minutes **makes** 1 cup (250ml)
nutritional count per 250ml 0.3g total fat (0.6g saturated fat);
314kJ (75 cal); 13.7g carbohydrate; 1.9g protein; 4.1g fibre

fast
lunches

Turkish chicken club sandwich

You will need to buy two butter lettuces for this recipe.

⅓ cup (80ml) lime juice
2 tablespoons olive oil
2 teaspoons sumac
2 chicken thigh fillets (400g)
1 large turkish bread (430g)
1 lebanese cucumber (130g), sliced thinly
1 medium tomato (150g), sliced thinly
24 small butter lettuce leaves
coriander aïoli
½ cup (150g) mayonnaise
1 tablespoon lime juice
1 clove garlic, crushed
2 tablespoons finely chopped fresh coriander

1 Combine juice, oil, sumac and chicken in medium bowl; stand
5 minutes.
2 Meanwhile, make coriander aïoli.
3 Drain chicken; reserve marinade. Cook chicken on heated oiled grill
plate (or grill or barbecue) until cooked through, brushing with reserved
marinade after turning. Cover; stand 5 minutes then slice thinly.
4 Halve bread horizontally; cut each piece into six slices. Toast slices lightly.
5 Spread each toast slice with aïoli. Layer four toast slices with half the
chicken, cucumber, tomato and lettuce; top with toasts then layer with
remaining chicken, cucumber, tomato and lettuce and top with remaining
toast. Cut in half to serve.
coriander aïoli Combine ingredients in small bowl.

preparation time 15 minutes **cooking time** 15 minutes **makes** 4
nutritional count per sandwich 32.1g total fat (5.4g saturated fat);
2700kJ (646 cal); 57.5g carbohydrate; 29.6g protein; 4.6g fibre

Soup with pistou

1 tablespoon olive oil
1 small brown onion (80g), chopped finely
2 cloves garlic, sliced thinly
1 large carrot (180g), chopped finely
1 stalk celery (150g), trimmed, chopped finely
1 medium potato (200g), cut into 1cm cubes
⅓ cup (75g) risoni
3 cups (750ml) chicken stock
1 cup (250ml) water
400g can white beans, rinsed, drained
2 tablespoons lemon juice
⅓ cup (90g) basil pesto

1 Heat oil in large saucepan, add onion, garlic, carrot and celery; cook, stirring, until onion softens. Add potato, risoni, stock and the water; bring to the boil. Reduce heat; cook about 10 minutes or until risoni is tender.
2 Add beans to pan; cook, stirring, uncovered, 1 minute.
3 Remove from heat; stir in juice. Serve with basil pesto.

preparation time 10 minutes **cooking time** 25 minutes **serves** 4
nutritional count per serving 14.8g total fat (3g saturated fat);
1342kJ (321 cal); 31.4g carbohydrate; 12g protein; 7.5g fibre

Roasted eggplant and chorizo pizza

We used small (15cm diameter) packaged pizza bases for this recipe.

4 x 112g pizza bases
⅓ cup (90g) sun-dried tomato pesto
320g jar char-grilled eggplant in oil, drained, chopped coarsely
½ cup (75g) seeded kalamata olives
1 chorizo sausage (170g), sliced thinly
½ cup (50g) coarsely grated pizza cheese
¼ cup loosely packed fresh oregano leaves

1 Preheat oven to 220°C/200°C fan-forced.
2 Place pizza bases on oven trays. Spread bases with pesto; top with eggplant, olives and chorizo, sprinkle with cheese. Cook, uncovered, about 15 minutes.
3 Sprinkle pizzas with oregano before serving.

preparation time 10 minutes **cooking time** 15 minutes **serves** 4
nutritional count per serving 40.7g total fat (16.3g saturated fat); 3089kJ (739 cal); 66.2g carbohydrate; 25g protein; 5.1g fibre

Egg drop soup

1 litre (4 cups) water
1 litre (4 cups) chicken stock
1 tablespoon light soy sauce
1 tablespoon chinese cooking wine
1 clove garlic, crushed
5cm piece fresh ginger (25g), grated
400g chicken breast fillets
3 eggs, beaten lightly
125g rice vermicelli, soaked, drained
¼ cup loosely packed fresh coriander leaves
1 green onion, cut diagonally
2 tablespoons coarsely chopped unsalted roasted peanuts

1 Bring the water, stock, sauce, wine, garlic and ginger to the boil in large saucepan; add chicken, return to the boil. Reduce heat; simmer, covered, about 10 minutes or until chicken is cooked. Remove chicken from broth; using two forks, shred meat.
2 Gradually whisk egg into the broth in a steady stream. Return chicken to pan.
3 Divide noodles among serving bowls; ladle soup into bowls, then sprinkle with coriander, onion and nuts.

preparation time 10 minutes **cooking time** 20 minutes **serves** 4
nutritional count per serving 15.1g total fat (4.1g saturated fat); 1551kJ (371 cal); 24.2g carbohydrate; 33.1g protein; 1.4g fibre

Smoked chicken, radicchio and basil leaf salad

340g asparagus, trimmed, chopped coarsely
500g smoked chicken breast fillets, sliced thickly
2 medium radicchio (400g), trimmed, leaves torn
⅔ cup loosely packed fresh basil leaves
pesto dressing
2 teaspoons basil pesto
¼ cup (60ml) balsamic vinegar
¼ cup (60ml) olive oil

1 Boil, steam or microwave asparagus until tender; drain. Rinse under cold water; drain.
2 Meanwhile, make pesto dressing.
3 Combine asparagus, dressing and remaining ingredients in large bowl.
pesto dressing Place ingredients in screw-top jar; shake well.

preparation time 10 minutes **cooking time** 5 minutes **serves** 4
nutritional count per serving 23.8g total fat (4.6g saturated fat);
1513kJ (362 cal); 2g carbohydrate; 33.8g protein; 3.2g fibre

Pepperoni pizzetta

We used a small (15cm diameter) packaged pizza base for this recipe.

1 small pizza base (112g)
2 tablespoons tomato paste
40g pepperoni, sliced thinly
1 fresh small red thai chilli, sliced thinly
¼ cup (20g) flaked parmesan cheese
15g baby rocket leaves
2 teaspoons lemon juice

1 Preheat oven to 220°C/200°C fan-forced.
2 Place pizza base on oven tray. Spread base with paste; top with pepperoni then sprinkle with chilli. Cook, uncovered, about 8 minutes.
3 Combine cheese, rocket and juice in small bowl. Serve pizzetta topped with rocket salad.

preparation time 5 minutes **cooking time** 8 minutes **serves** 1
nutritional count per serving 25.4g total fat (9.9g saturated fat); 2592kJ (620 cal); 65.5g carbohydrate; 29g protein; 6.2g fibre

Beef burgers

1 small red onion (100g), halved
500g beef mince
1 tablespoon tomato sauce
½ cup (125ml) barbecue sauce
4 thin slices fresh pineapple (150g)
4 hamburger buns (360g)
1½ cups finely shredded iceberg lettuce
1 large tomato (220g), sliced thinly
225g can beetroot slices, drained

1 Chop half the onion finely; cut remaining half into four slices.
2 Combine mince, tomato sauce, 1 tablespoon of the barbecue sauce and chopped onion in medium bowl. Shape mixture into four patties.
3 Cook pineapple slices and onion slices on heated oiled grill plate (or grill or barbecue) until pineapple is browned. Cook patties.
4 Preheat grill. Split buns; toast cut sides under grill.
5 Spread remaining barbecue sauce on bun bases; layer all ingredients between bun halves.

preparation time 15 minutes **cooking time** 15 minutes **serves** 4
nutritional count per serving 12.3g total fat (4.1g saturated fat); 2337kJ (559 cal); 71.8g carbohydrate; 35.7g protein; 6.9g fibre

Potato and bacon pizza

It's important to slice the potatoes as thinly as possible.

4 x 115g individual pizza bases
2 tablespoons olive oil
4 rindless bacon rashers (260g), chopped coarsely
2 cloves garlic, sliced thinly
1 tablespoon coarsely chopped fresh rosemary
½ teaspoon dried chilli flakes
500g potatoes, sliced thinly
1 cup (80g) finely grated parmesan cheese

1 Preheat oven to 220°C/200°C fan-forced.
2 Place pizza bases on oven trays; bake about 10 minutes or until crisp.
3 Meanwhile, heat oil in large frying pan; cook bacon, garlic, rosemary and chilli, stirring, 5 minutes. Remove mixture from pan.
4 Add potato to same heated pan; cook, stirring frequently, about 10 minutes or until tender.
5 Sprinkle each pizza base with ¼ cup of the cheese. Divide potato and bacon mixture among bases. Bake about 5 minutes.

preparation time 15 minutes **cooking time** 20 minutes **serves** 4
nutritional count per serving 25.7g total fat (7.6g saturated fat); 3486kJ (834 cal); 105.6g carbohydrate; 39.6g protein; 9g fibre

Turkish lamb and yogurt salad

600g lamb backstrap
2 tablespoons sumac
1 tablespoon olive oil
¼ cup (70g) yogurt
2 tablespoons lemon juice
250g cherry tomatoes, halved
2 lebanese cucumbers (260g), seeded, sliced thinly
½ cup loosely packed fresh flat-leaf parsley leaves
½ cup loosely packed fresh mint leaves
1 small red onion (100g), sliced thinly

1 Rub lamb with sumac. Heat oil in large frying pan; cook lamb, uncovered, until cooked as desired. Cover lamb; stand 5 minutes then slice thinly.
2 Meanwhile, whisk yogurt and juice in small jug.
3 Combine lamb and remaining ingredients in large bowl; pour over dressing.

preparation time 15 minutes **cooking time** 10 minutes **serves** 4
nutritional count per serving 10.8g total fat (3.4g saturated fat);
1062kJ (254 cal); 5.1g carbohydrate; 32.9g protein; 2.7g fibre

Fetta and artichoke pizzetta

We used a small (15cm diameter) packaged pizza base for this recipe.

1 small pizza base (112g)
50g soft fetta cheese, crumbled
1 teaspoon olive oil
1 marinated artichoke (70g), sliced thinly
1 tablespoon fresh oregano leaves
2 teaspoons lime juice

1 Preheat oven to 220°C/200°C fan-forced.
2 Place pizza base on oven tray. Combine 1 tablespoon of the cheese with oil. Spread pizza base with cheese paste; top with artichoke then sprinkle with remaining cheese. Cook, uncovered, about 8 minutes.
3 Serve pizzetta sprinkled with oregano and juice.

preparation time 5 minutes **cooking time** 8 minutes **serves** 1
nutritional count per serving 22g total fat (9.2g saturated fat);
2223kJ (532 cal); 60.8g carbohydrate; 20.3g protein; 4.2g fibre

Corn and goat cheese quesadillas

You need to buy 2 untrimmed corn cobs (800g) to get the amount of trimmed corn needed for this recipe.

2 trimmed corn cobs (500g)
240g soft goats cheese
8 large (20cm) flour tortillas
½ cup (100g) char-grilled capsicum, sliced thinly
40g jalapeño chilli slices, drained
⅓ cup coarsely chopped fresh coriander
20g butter
40g baby spinach leaves
1 lime, cut into wedges

1 Cook cobs on heated oiled grill plate (or grill or barbecue) until kernels are tender and browned lightly; when cool enough to handle, cut kernels from cobs.
2 Spread cheese lightly over tortillas. Top four tortillas with corn, capsicum, chilli and coriander; top with remaining tortillas. Press around edges firmly to seal quesadillas.
3 Heat butter in medium frying pan; cook quesadillas, one at a time, until browned both sides and heated through.
4 Serve quesadillas with spinach and wedges.

preparation time 10 minutes **cooking time** 20 minutes **serves** 4
nutritional count per serving 21.7g total fat (10g saturated fat);
2169kJ (519 cal); 57g carbohydrate; 19.8g protein; 8.6g fibre

Grilled steak and vegie-salsa sandwich

1 medium red capsicum (200g), chopped coarsely
1 small zucchini (90g), chopped coarsely
1 medium red onion (170g), chopped coarsely
2 tablespoons bottled chunky tomato salsa
4 beef minute steaks (400g)
4 wholemeal hamburger buns (360g)
1 tablespoon olive oil
40g mesclun
120g bocconcini cheese, sliced thickly

1 Cook capsicum, zucchini and onion on heated oiled grill plate
(or grill or barbecue) until tender; combine with salsa in small bowl.
2 Cook steak on heated oiled grill plate (or grill or barbecue) until
cooked as desired.
3 Preheat grill. Meanwhile, halve buns horizontally; brush cut-sides
with oil. Toast bun halves, cut-sides up, under grill.
4 Place mesclun and vegie-salsa on bottom halves of buns; top with
steaks then cheese. Grill about 2 minutes or until cheese melts. Top
with remaining bun halves.

preparation time 5 minutes **cooking time** 25 minutes **serves** 4
nutritional count per serving 18.8g total fat (6.6g saturated fat);
2245kJ (537 cal); 52.8g carbohydrate; 36.2g protein; 5.1g fibre

Croque madame

8 slices wholemeal bread (360g)
8 slices leg ham (240g)
40g butter
4 eggs
cheese béchamel
20g butter
1 tablespoon plain flour
¾ cup (180ml) milk
½ cup (60g) finely grated cheddar cheese
1 tablespoon finely chopped fresh flat-leaf parsley

1 Make cheese béchamel.
2 Spread béchamel onto bread slices. Top four slices with ham then remaining bread.
3 Melt butter in large frying pan. Add sandwiches; fry, in batches, until browned both sides.
4 Fry eggs in same pan until cooked. Top each sandwich with an egg.
cheese béchamel Melt butter in small saucepan, add flour; cook, stirring, until mixture bubbles and thickens. Gradually add milk; cook, stirring, until sauce boils and thickens. Remove from heat; stir in cheese and parsley.

preparation time 15 minutes **cooking time** 20 minutes **serves** 4
nutritional count per serving 29.2g total fat (15.2g saturated fat); 2328kJ (557 cal); 38.6g carbohydrate; 32.3g protein; 5.8g fibre

Italian chicken patties on focaccia

500g chicken mince
1/3 cup (50g) drained semi-dried tomatoes, chopped finely
1/2 small brown onion (40g), chopped finely
1/4 cup (20g) coarsely grated parmesan cheese
2 tablespoons finely chopped fresh flat-leaf parsley
4 slices pancetta (60g)
4 focaccia rolls (440g)
1/2 cup (160g) tomato chutney
40g mixed baby salad leaves
1 large tomato (220g), sliced thinly

1 Combine mince, semi-dried tomato, onion, cheese and parsley in medium bowl. Shape mixture into four patties.
2 Cook pancetta in heated large frying pan until crisp; remove from pan. Cook patties in same pan.
3 Preheat grill. Split rolls; toast cut sides under grill.
4 Spread chutney on roll bases; sandwich leaves, tomato, patties and pancetta between roll halves.

preparation time 15 minutes **cooking time** 15 minutes **serves** 4
nutritional count per serving 18.6g total fat (5.5g saturated fat);
2667kJ (638 cal); 72.4g carbohydrate; 41g protein; 6.6g fibre

Orange, beetroot and roast beef salad

2 medium oranges (480g)
400g shaved rare roast beef
850g can whole baby beetroot, drained, halved
150g baby rocket leaves
½ cup (125ml) buttermilk
¼ cup (75g) mayonnaise
1 tablespoon wholegrain mustard
100g blue cheese, crumbled

1 Segment oranges over large bowl; reserve 1 tablespoon juice separately.
2 Add beef, beetroot and rocket to bowl.
3 Whisk reserved juice with buttermilk, mayonnaise and mustard in small bowl.
4 Sprinkle cheese over salad; drizzle with dressing.

preparation time 15 minutes **serves** 4
nutritional count per serving 19.9g total fat (8.4g saturated fat); 1860kJ (445 cal); 26.8g carbohydrate; 36.4g protein; 6.2g fibre

Kumara, rosemary and caramelised onion pizza

2 tablespoons olive oil
1 large kumara (500g), chopped coarsely
2 cloves garlic, crushed
1 tablespoon finely chopped fresh rosemary
1 teaspoon chilli flakes
40g butter
1 large red onion (300g), sliced thinly
4 large pitta breads (320g)
1 cup (260g) bottled tomato pasta sauce
2 cups (200g) coarsely grated mozzarella cheese
½ cup loosely packed fresh mint leaves

1 Preheat oven to 240°C/220°C fan-forced.
2 Combine oil, kumara, garlic, rosemary and chilli in medium shallow baking dish. Roast, uncovered, about 15 minutes or until kumara is tender.
3 Meanwhile, melt butter in medium frying pan; cook onion, stirring occasionally, about 15 minutes or until caramelised.
4 Place pitta on oven trays; spread with pasta sauce. Divide kumara and onion among pitta; sprinkle with cheese. Cook, uncovered, about 10 minutes or until pitta bases are crisp and topping is heated through; serve sprinkled with mint.

preparation time 10 minutes **cooking time** 25 minutes **serves** 4
nutritional count per serving 31g total fat (14.1g saturated fat); 2780kJ (665 cal); 68.8g carbohydrate; 25g protein; 7.3g fibre

Tomato, pesto and olive tart

500g grape tomatoes
1 tablespoon balsamic vinegar
1 tablespoon olive oil
1 sheet ready-rolled puff pasty
2 tablespoons basil pesto
⅓ cup (55g) seeded black olives
1½ cups (360g) ricotta cheese

1 Preheat oven to 220°C/200°C fan-forced.
2 Combine tomatoes in medium bowl with vinegar and half the oil; place on oven tray. Roast, uncovered, about 10 minutes or until tomatoes collapse.
3 Place pastry on oiled oven tray. Fold edges of pastry over to make a 5mm border all the way around pastry; prick base with fork. Place another oven tray on top of pastry (to stop pastry puffing up); bake 10 minutes. Remove top tray from pastry; reduce temperature to 200°C/180°C fan-forced.
4 Spread pastry with pesto; top with tomatoes and olives. Sprinkle with cheese. Bake about 10 minutes. Drizzle with remaining oil before serving.

preparation time 10 minutes **cooking time** 20 minutes **serves** 4
nutritional count per serving 28.4g total fat (13.1g saturated fat); 1672kJ (400 cal); 22g carbohydrate; 13.5g protein; 2.9g fibre

Moroccan pizzetta

We used a small (15cm diameter) packaged pizza base for this recipe. You need to buy half a small barbecued chicken (480g) for this recipe.

1 small pizza base (112g)
2 tablespoons hummus
½ cup (80g) shredded barbecued chicken
30g preserved lemon, rinsed, sliced thinly
30g haloumi cheese, sliced thinly
1 tablespoon fresh flat-leaf parsley leaves
1 teaspoon olive oil

1 Preheat oven to 220°C/200°C fan-forced.
2 Place pizza base on oven tray. Spread base with hummus; top with chicken, lemon then cheese. Cook, uncovered, about 8 minutes.
3 Serve pizzetta sprinkled with parsley and oil.

preparation time 5 minutes **cooking time** 8 minutes **serves** 1
nutritional count per serving 22.7g total fat (7g saturated fat); 2679kJ (641 cal); 64.3g carbohydrate; 40.2g protein; 8.6g fibre

Ham, sage and fontina pizza

We used large (25cm diameter) packaged pizza bases for this recipe.
Substitute the fontina with mozzarella cheese, if you prefer.

2 x 335g pizza bases
1 tablespoon olive oil
2 cloves garlic, crushed
2 tablespoons finely chopped fresh sage
100g thinly sliced ham
200g fontina cheese, sliced thinly

1 Preheat oven to 220°C/200°C fan-forced.
2 Place pizza bases on oven trays. Spread bases with combined oil, garlic and sage; top with ham and cheese. Cook, uncovered, about 10 minutes.

preparation time 10 minutes **cooking time** 10 minutes **serves** 4
nutritional count per serving 26.8g total fat (11.3g saturated fat);
3110kJ (744 cal); 89g carbohydrate; 33g protein; 6.5g fibre

Lemon salmon patties on turkish bread

500g pontiac potatoes, chopped coarsely
415g can pink salmon, drained
1 egg
2 green onions, chopped finely
1 teaspoon finely grated lemon rind
1 lebanese cucumber (130g)
1 large loaf turkish bread (430g), cut into quarters
⅓ cup (80ml) sweet chilli sauce
40g mizuna

1 Boil, steam or microwave potato until tender; drain; mash potato.
2 Combine salmon, egg, onion and rind in medium bowl with potato. Shape mixture into four patties.
3 Cook patties in heated oiled large frying pan.
4 Using a vegetable peeler, slice cucumber into ribbons.
5 Preheat grill. Split bread; toast cut sides under grill.
6 Spread sauce on bread bases; sandwich cucumber, mizuna and patties between bread slices.

preparation time 15 minutes **cooking time** 20 minutes **serves** 4
nutritional count per serving 10.6g total fat (2.5g saturated fat); 2203kJ (527 cal); 70.3g carbohydrate; 33.5g protein; 6.2g fibre

Salami, bocconcini and pasta salad

500g mini penne pasta
½ cup (75g) seeded black olives, halved
250g cherry tomatoes, halved
180g bocconcini cheese, halved
100g spicy salami, chopped coarsely
1 cup firmly packed fresh basil leaves
red wine vinaigrette
⅓ cup (80ml) olive oil
¼ cup (60ml) red wine vinegar
2 teaspoons dijon mustard
1 clove garlic, crushed

1 Cook pasta in large saucepan of boiling water, uncovered, until just tender; drain. Rinse under cold water; drain.
2 Meanwhile, make red wine vinaigrette.
3 Combine pasta, vinaigrette and remaining ingredients in large bowl.
red wine vinaigrette Place ingredients in screw-top jar; shake well.

preparation time 10 minutes **cooking time** 15 minutes **serves** 6
nutritional count per serving 24.1g total fat (4.9g saturated fat); 2274kJ (544 cal); 61g carbohydrate; 18.6g protein; 3.9g fibre

Spinach and beetroot tart

1 sheet ready-rolled puff pasty
250g frozen spinach, thawed, drained
1 cup (200g) fetta cheese, crumbled
½ x 850g can drained baby beetroot, sliced thinly

1 Preheat oven to 220°C/200°C fan-forced.
2 Place pastry on an oiled oven tray. Fold edges of pastry over to make a 5mm border all the way around pastry. Prick pastry base with fork. Place another oven tray on top of pastry (to stop pastry from puffing up); bake 10 minutes. Remove top tray from pastry; reduce oven temperature to 200°C/180°C fan-forced.
3 Meanwhile, combine spinach with half the cheese in medium bowl.
4 Top tart with spinach mixture, beetroot and remaining cheese.
5 Bake tart about 10 minutes.

preparation time 10 minutes **cooking time** 20 minutes **serves** 4
nutritional count per serving 21.4g total fat (12.8g saturated fat);
1421kJ (340 cal); 22.1g carbohydrate; 13.4g protein; 4g fibre

Coppa and ricotta panini

We used coppa in this sandwich, but you can use parma ham or prosciutto, if you prefer.

⅓ cup (80g) black olive tapenade
¼ cup (60ml) balsamic vinegar
4 focaccia rolls (440g), halved
240g ricotta cheese
½ teaspoon finely grated lemon rind
1 teaspoon lemon juice
16 slices coppa (240g)
40g baby rocket leaves

1 Combine tapenade with 2 tablespoons of the vinegar in small bowl; spread over bottom half of each roll.
2 Combine cheese with rind and juice in small bowl; spread over tapenade then top with coppa and rocket and drizzle with remaining vinegar. Top with remaining roll halves.
3 Preheat sandwich press.
4 Cook panini in sandwich press until browned lightly and heated through.

preparation time 10 minutes **cooking time** 20 minutes **serves** 4
nutritional count per serving 18.2g total fat (6.7g saturated fat); 2036kJ (487 cal); 51.3g carbohydrate; 27.6g protein; 3g fibre

Felafel

2 x 400g cans chickpeas, rinsed, drained
1 clove garlic, chopped coarsely
1 small brown onion (80g), chopped coarsely
1 tablespoon olive oil
1 egg
2 teaspoons ground cumin
½ teaspoon bicarbonate of soda
2 tablespoons plain flour
vegetable oil, for shallow-frying
4 large pitta breads (320g), warmed
yogurt sauce
1 cup (280g) yogurt
½ clove garlic, crushed
1 tablespoon lemon juice
½ teaspoon cayenne pepper

1 Process chickpeas, garlic, onion and olive oil until ingredients begin to combine; transfer mixture to medium bowl. Stir in egg, cumin, soda and flour until combined. Shape mixture into 12 patties.
2 Heat vegetable oil in large frying pan; cook felafel, in batches, until browned. Drain on absorbent paper.
3 Meanwhile, make yogurt sauce.
4 Serve felafel on pitta, topped with yogurt sauce. Serve the felafel with a rocket and tomato salad, if you like.
yogurt sauce Combine ingredients in small bowl.

preparation time 15 minutes **cooking time** 10 minutes **serves** 4
nutritional count per serving 21.8g total fat (4.3g saturated fat); 2416kJ (575 cal); 68.3g carbohydrate; 21.7g protein; 9.1g fibre

Pizzetta caprese

We used a small (15cm diameter) packaged pizza base for this recipe.

1 small pizza base (112g)
2 cherry bocconcini cheeses (30g), sliced thinly
½ clove garlic, sliced thinly
1 small tomato (90g), sliced thinly
1 tablespoon fresh basil leaves

1 Preheat oven to 220°C/200°C fan-forced.
2 Place pizza base on oven tray. Top base with cheese and garlic; cook, uncovered, about 8 minutes.
3 Serve pizzetta topped with tomato and basil.

preparation time 5 minutes **cooking time** 8 minutes **serves** 1
nutritional count per serving 9g total fat (3.6g saturated fat); 1693kJ (405 cal); 61.3g carbohydrate; 16.3g protein; 5.6g fibre

Pitta filled with lamb and tabbouleh

¾ cup (200g) low-fat yogurt
2 cloves garlic, crushed
500g lamb mince
1 teaspoon ground cumin
1 teaspoon ground coriander
½ small brown onion (40g), chopped finely
1 egg
4 pitta pocket breads (340g)
½ baby cos lettuce (90g), leaves separated
⅔ cup (115g) tabbouleh

1 Combine yogurt and half the garlic in small bowl.
2 Combine remaining garlic, mince, spices, onion and egg in medium bowl. Shape into eight patties. Cook patties in heated oiled large frying pan.
3 Split pitta not quite through; fill pockets with lettuce, tabbouleh, patties and yogurt.

preparation time 15 minutes **cooking time** 15 minutes **serves** 4
nutritional count per serving 15.7g total fat (5.2g saturated fat); 2132kJ (510 cal); 49.9g carbohydrate; 39.3g protein; 4.7g fibre

Smoked cheese and sopressa pizza

We used large (25cm diameter) packaged pizza bases for this recipe.

2 x 335g pizza bases
½ cup (140g) tomato paste
100g hot sopressa salami, sliced thinly
1 cup (150g) semi-dried tomatoes, drained, chopped coarsely
100g smoked cheddar cheese, flaked
50g baby rocket leaves

1 Preheat oven to 220°C/200°C fan-forced.
2 Place pizza bases on oven trays. Spread bases with paste; top with sopressa and tomato. Cook, uncovered, about 15 minutes.
3 Top pizzas with cheese and rocket.

preparation time 10 minutes **cooking time** 15 minutes **serves** 4
nutritional count per serving 24.6g total fat (5.4g saturated fat);
3352kJ (802 cal); 106.3g carbohydrate; 31.5g protein; 13.3g fibre

fast
after school

Ham, egg and cheese toastie

2 slices wholemeal bread (90g)
1 tablespoon barbecue sauce
30g shaved ham
1 hard-boiled egg, sliced
¼ cup (30g) coarsely grated reduced-fat cheddar cheese

1 Preheat sandwich press.
2 Spread bread with sauce; top one bread slice with ham, egg and cheese then remaining bread slice.
3 Toast in sandwich press until golden brown. Cut in half to serve.

preparation time 5 minutes **cooking time** 5 minutes **serves** 1
nutritional count per serving 16.1g total fat (6.9g saturated fat);
1898kJ (454 cal); 44.3g carbohydrate; 29.7g protein; 5.9g fibre

Strawberry soy smoothie

5 strawberries (100g), hulled, halved
½ cup (125ml) chilled strawberry soy milk
½ cup (125ml) strawberry soy ice-cream

1 Blend or process ingredients until smooth.
2 Pour into glass; serve immediately.

preparation time 5 minutes **makes** 1 cup (250ml)
nutritional count per 250ml 5.6g total fat (0.6g saturated fat);
744kJ (178 cal); 24.7g carbohydrate; 5g protein; 4.2g fibre

Pizza mexicana

1 pocket pitta bread (85g)
¼ cup (60g) canned refried beans
¼ small red capsicum (35g), chopped finely
2 teaspoons sweet chilli sauce
2 tablespoons pizza cheese
1 green onion, sliced thinly

1 Preheat oven to 180°C/160°C fan-forced.
2 Place pitta on oven tray. Spread pitta with beans; top with capsicum, sauce and cheese. Cook, uncovered, about 15 minutes or until cheese melts.
3 Sprinkle onion over pizza just before serving.

preparation time 5 minutes **cooking time** 15 minutes **serves** 1
nutritional count per serving 9.5g total fat (4.7g saturated fat); 1689kJ (404 cal); 54.7g carbohydrate; 21g protein; 6.6g fibre

Buttermilk fruit smoothie

Freeze unpeeled bananas then use them straight from the freezer
to give your smoothie an ice-creamy texture.

1 small pear (180g), cored, chopped coarsely
1 small banana (130g), chopped coarsely
2 teaspoons honey
½ cup (125ml) buttermilk
½ cup (125ml) chilled apple juice

1 Blend or process ingredients until smooth.
2 Pour into glass; serve with ice.

preparation time 5 minutes **makes** 1 cup (250ml)
nutritional count per serving 2.8g total fat (1.7g saturated fat);
1488kJ (356 cal); 71.2g carbohydrate; 7.5g protein; 6g fibre

Pesto, ham and mushroom pizza

3 large button mushrooms (30g), chopped finely
1 tablespoon basil pesto
1 pocket pitta bread (85g)
25g ham, chopped finely
1 tablespoon pizza cheese
2 tablespoons low-fat cottage cheese
1 tablespoon finely chopped fresh flat-leaf parsley

1 Preheat oven to 180°C/160°C fan-forced.
2 Combine mushrooms and pesto in small bowl.
3 Place pitta on oven tray. Spread pitta with mushroom mixture; top with ham and cheeses. Cook, uncovered, about 15 minutes or until cheese melts.
4 Sprinkle parsley over pizza just before serving.

preparation time 5 minutes **cooking time** 15 minutes **serves** 1
nutritional count per serving 15.6g total fat (5.4g saturated fat);
1848kJ (442 cal); 45.4g carbohydrate; 27.9g protein; 3.8g fibre

Choc-malt smoothie

½ cup (125ml) low-fat milk
1 cup (250ml) reduced-fat vanilla ice-cream
1 tablespoon malted milk powder
2 teaspoons chocolate-hazelnut spread
pinch ground cinnamon

1 Blend or process ingredients until smooth.
2 Pour into glass; serve immediately.

preparation time 5 minutes **makes** 1¼ cups (310ml)
nutritional count per 310ml 12.4g total fat (6.8g saturated fat);
1254kJ (360 cal); 47.8g carbohydrate; 13.9g protein; 0.1g fibre

Bruschetta fingers

1 small turkish bread roll (110g)
2 teaspoons sun-dried tomato pesto
6 cherry tomatoes (60g), quartered
30g baby bocconcini cheese, sliced thinly
1 tablespoon finely chopped fresh flat-leaf parsley

1 Split bread in half; toast cut sides, then cut into fingers.
2 Spread toast with pesto; top with tomato and cheese then sprinkle with parsley.

preparation time 5 minutes **cooking time** 5 minutes **serves** 1
nutritional count per serving 12.2g total fat (4.4g saturated fat); 1618kJ (387 cal); 50.6g carbohydrate; 16.3g protein; 4.3g fibre

Almond and berry smoothie

1 cup (250ml) chilled water
½ cup (70g) roasted slivered almonds
3 drops vanilla extract
⅓ cup (50g) frozen raspberries
¾ cup (180ml) reduced-fat frozen raspberry yogurt

1 Blend or process the water and nuts until smooth. Strain mixture into small jug; discard solids.
2 Return almond milk to blender with vanilla, raspberries and yogurt; blend until smooth.
3 Pour into glass; serve immediately.

preparation time 5 minutes **makes** 1 cup (250ml)
nutritional count per 250ml 7g total fat (4.5g saturated fat); 1630kJ (370 cal); 59g carbohydrate; 15.5g protein; 2.7g fibre

Pumpkin and fetta pizza

50g piece pumpkin
1 teaspoon olive oil
1 pocket pitta bread (85g)
2 tablespoons bottled tomato pasta sauce
25g reduced-fat fetta cheese, crumbled
2 teaspoons finely chopped fresh mint

1 Preheat oven to 180°C/160°C fan-forced.
2 Using vegetable peeler, slice pumpkin into thin strips. Combine pumpkin and oil in small bowl.
3 Place pitta on oven tray. Spread pitta with sauce; top with pumpkin and cheese. Cook, uncovered, about 15 minutes or until pumpkin is tender.
4 Serve pizza sprinkled with mint.

preparation time 10 minutes **cooking time** 15 minutes **serves** 1
nutritional count per serving 10.7g total fat (3.4g saturated fat);
1576kJ (377 cal); 51.6g carbohydrate; 16.1g protein; 3.9g fibre

Kiwifruit and mint frappé

4 medium kiwifruits (340g), peeled, chopped coarsely
¾ cup ice cubes
¼ cup (60ml) apple juice
¼ cup coarsely chopped fresh mint leaves
1 teaspoon caster sugar
1 teaspoon finely shredded fresh mint

1 Blend or process kiwifruit, ice, juice, chopped mint and sugar until smooth.
2 Pour into glass; top with shredded mint.

preparation time 5 minutes **makes** 1 ½ cups (375ml)
nutritional count per 375ml 0.8g total fat (0g saturated fat); 974kJ (233 cal); 44.8g carbohydrate; 5.2g protein; 12.2g fibre

Chicken quesadilla

2 large flour tortillas
40g packaged reduced-fat cream cheese
½ cup (80g) shredded barbecued chicken
¼ cup (35g) coarsely chopped drained semi-dried tomatoes
½ medium avocado (125g), mashed

1 Preheat sandwich press.
2 Place one tortilla on board; spread with cream cheese then top with chicken and tomato.
3 Spread second tortilla with avocado; place, avocado-side-down, on first tortilla.
4 Toast in sandwich press until golden brown. Cut quesadilla into quarters to serve.

preparation time 5 minutes **cooking time** 5 minutes **serves** 1
nutritional count per serving 41.2g total fat (11.6g saturated fat);
3265kJ (781 cal); 61.8g carbohydrate; 36.5g protein; 9.1g fibre

Bacon and corn pizza

1 pocket pitta bread (85g)
1 tablespoon corn relish
1 rindless bacon rasher (65g), chopped finely
2 tablespoons pizza cheese
1 tablespoon finely chopped fresh flat-leaf parsley

1 Preheat oven to 180°C/160°C fan-forced.
2 Place pitta on oven tray. Spread pitta with relish; top with bacon and cheese. Cook, uncovered, about 15 minutes or until bacon crisps and cheese melts.
3 Sprinkle parsley over pizza just before serving.

preparation time 5 minutes **cooking time** 15 minutes **serves** 1
nutritional count per serving 17.3g total fat (7.7g saturated fat); 2027kJ (485 cal); 50.5g carbohydrate; 29.7g protein; 3g fibre

Turkey on toasted turkish bread

1 small turkish bread roll (110g)
1 tablespoon cranberry sauce
30g shaved turkey
10g shaved reduced-fat jarlsberg cheese
10g baby spinach leaves

1 Preheat sandwich press.
2 Split bread in half. Spread sauce onto cut sides then sandwich turkey, cheese and spinach between pieces.
3 Toast in sandwich press until golden brown.

preparation time 5 minutes **cooking time** 5 minutes **serves** 1
nutritional count per serving 7g total fat (2.2g saturated fat); 1659kJ (397 cal); 58.5g carbohydrate; 22.4g protein; 3.1g fibre

fast
afternoons

White chocolate macadamia cookies

1½ cups (225g) plain flour
½ teaspoon bicarbonate of soda
¼ cup (55g) caster sugar
⅓ cup (75g) firmly packed brown sugar
125g butter, melted
½ teaspoon vanilla extract
1 egg
180g white eating chocolate, chopped coarsely
¾ cup (105g) roasted macadamias, chopped coarsely

1 Preheat oven to 200°C/180°C fan-forced. Grease two oven trays;
line with baking paper.
2 Sift flour, soda and sugars into large bowl. Stir in butter, extract and
egg then chocolate and nuts. Drop rounded tablespoons of mixture,
5cm apart on trays.
3 Bake cookies about 10 minutes. Cool on trays.

preparation time 10 minutes **cooking time** 10 minutes **makes** 24
nutritional count per cookie 10.4g total fat (4.9g saturated fat);
706kJ (169 cal); 16.4g carbohydrate; 2.2g protein; 0.6g fibre

Berry yogurt muffins

We used a mixture of raspberries and blueberries in these muffins.

1½ cups (225g) self-raising flour
⅓ cup (30g) rolled oats
3 eggs
¾ cup (165g) firmly packed brown sugar
¾ cup (200g) yogurt
⅓ cup (80ml) vegetable oil
180g fresh or frozen berries

1 Preheat oven to 200°C/180°C fan-forced. Grease six-hole texas (¾-cup/180ml) muffin pan.
2 Combine sifted flour with oats in medium bowl. Stir in eggs, sugar, yogurt and oil; add berries, stir gently into muffin mixture.
3 Spoon mixture into pan holes; bake about 20 minutes. Stand 5 minutes before turning, top-side up, onto wire rack to cool.

preparation time 10 minutes **cooking time** 20 minutes **makes** 6
nutritional count per muffin 16.9g total fat (3.2g saturated fat); 1806kJ (432 cal); 58.8g carbohydrate; 9.7g protein; 2.5g fibre

Scones with strawberries and cream

3 cups (450g) self-raising flour
2 tablespoons caster sugar
40g cold butter, chopped
2 cups (500ml) buttermilk
2 tablespoons buttermilk, extra
250g strawberries, halved
300ml thickened cream, whipped

1 Preheat oven to 240°C/220°C fan-forced. Grease 20cm x 30cm lamington pan.
2 Sift flour and sugar into large bowl; rub in butter with fingertips. Add buttermilk; use knife to "cut" buttermilk through the mixture to form a soft, sticky dough. Knead dough lightly on floured surface until smooth.
3 Press dough out to an even 2.5cm thickness. Dip 6.5cm cutter into flour; cut as many rounds as possible from the dough. Place scones side by side, just touching, in pan.
4 Gently knead scraps of dough together; repeat pressing and cutting of dough, place in pan. Brush tops with extra buttermilk; bake about 20 minutes or until scones sound hollow when tapped firmly on the top.
5 Serve scones with strawberries and cream.

preparation time 15 minutes **cooking time** 20 minutes **makes** 15
nutritional count per scone 9.9g total fat (6.3g saturated fat); 869kJ (208 cal); 24.4g carbohydrate; 4.8g protein; 1.4g fibre

Polenta and orange biscuits

125g butter, softened
2 teaspoons finely grated orange rind
⅔ cup (110g) icing sugar
⅓ cup (55g) polenta
1 cup (150g) plain flour

1 Preheat oven to 180°C/160°C fan-forced. Grease oven trays; line with baking paper.
2 Beat butter, rind and sifted icing sugar in small bowl with electric mixer until just combined; stir in polenta and sifted flour. Shape mixture into 30cm-rectangular log; cut log into 1cm slices. Place slices on trays 2cm apart.
3 Bake biscuits about 15 minutes. Stand biscuits on trays 5 minutes; transfer to wire rack to cool.

preparation time 15 minutes **cooking time** 15 minutes **makes** 30
nutritional count per biscuit 3.5g total fat (2.3g saturated fat); 288kJ (69 cal); 8.6g carbohydrate; 0.7g protein; 0.2g fibre

Banana, date and rolled oat cookies

You need 1 overripe medium banana (230g) for this recipe.

125g butter, softened
1 teaspoon finely grated lemon rind
1 cup (220g) firmly packed brown sugar
1 egg yolk
⅓ cup mashed banana
1½ cups (225g) plain flour
½ teaspoon bicarbonate of soda
1 cup (90g) rolled oats
½ cup (75g) finely chopped dried dates
⅔ cup (60g) rolled oats, extra
4 dried dates (35g), seeded, chopped coarsely

1 Preheat oven to 180°C/160°C fan-forced. Grease oven trays; line with baking paper.
2 Beat butter, rind, sugar and egg yolk in small bowl with electric mixer until combined; stir in banana then sifted flour and soda, oats and dates.
3 Roll level tablespoons of mixture into balls; roll each ball in extra oats then place on trays 5cm apart. Press a piece of coarsely chopped date into centre of each ball.
4 Bake cookies about 15 minutes. Cool cookies on trays.

preparation time 20 minutes **cooking time** 15 minutes **makes** 28
nutritional count per cookie 4.4g total fat (2.6g saturated fat);
539kJ (129 cal); 19.9g carbohydrate; 1.7g protein; 1.7g fibre

Cranberry and coconut biscuits

200g butter, softened
½ teaspoon vanilla extract
1 cup (160g) icing sugar
1 egg
½ cup (65g) dried cranberries
½ cup (40g) shredded coconut
1¾ cups (260g) plain flour
½ teaspoon bicarbonate of soda

1 Preheat oven to 180°C/160°C fan-forced. Grease oven trays; line with baking paper.
2 Beat butter, extract, sifted icing sugar and egg in small bowl with electric mixer until light and fluffy. Transfer to medium bowl; stir in cranberries and coconut. Stir in sifted flour and soda, in two batches.
3 Roll level tablespoons of dough into balls; place on trays 3cm apart.
4 Bake biscuits about 15 minutes. Cool biscuits on trays.

preparation time 20 minutes **cooking time** 15 minutes **makes** 30
nutritional count per biscuit 6.6g total fat (4.4g saturated fat);
497kJ (119 cal); 13.2g carbohydrate; 1.3g protein; 0.6g fibre

Lemon and coconut friands

6 egg whites
185g butter, melted
1 cup (100g) hazelnut meal
1½ cups (240g) icing sugar
½ cup (75g) plain flour
2 teaspoons finely grated lemon rind
1 tablespoon lemon juice
¼ cup (20g) desiccated coconut
⅓ cup (15g) flaked coconut

1 Preheat oven to 200°C/180°C fan-forced. Grease 12-hole
(⅓-cup/80ml) muffin pan.
2 Whisk egg whites with a fork in medium bowl until frothy. Add butter, meal, sifted icing sugar and flour, rind, juice and desiccated coconut; stir until combined.
3 Place ¼-cups of mixture into pan holes; sprinkle with flaked coconut.
4 Bake friands about 20 minutes. Stand 5 minutes before turning, top-side up, onto wire rack to cool.

preparation time 15 minutes **cooking time** 20 minutes **makes** 12
nutritional count per friand 19.7g total fat (10.2g saturated fat);
1237kJ (296 cal); 25.3g carbohydrate; 4g protein; 1.6g fibre

Brown sugar and pecan biscuits

200g butter, softened
½ teaspoon vanilla extract
1 cup (220g) firmly packed brown sugar
1 egg
½ cup (60g) coarsely chopped pecans
1¾ cups (260g) plain flour
½ teaspoon bicarbonate of soda

1 Preheat oven to 180°C/160°C fan-forced. Grease oven trays; line with baking paper.
2 Beat butter, extract, sugar and egg in small bowl with electric mixer until light and fluffy. Transfer to medium bowl; stir in nuts then sifted flour and soda, in two batches.
3 Roll level tablespoons of dough into balls; place on trays 3cm apart.
4 Bake biscuits about 15 minutes. Cool biscuits on trays.

preparation time 20 minutes **cooking time** 15 minutes **makes** 30
nutritional count per biscuit 7.2g total fat (3.8g saturated fat);
523kJ (125 cal); 13.5g carbohydrate; 1.4g protein; 1.5g fibre

Coffee almond biscuits

1 tablespoon instant coffee granules
3 teaspoons hot water
3 cups (360g) almond meal
1 cup (220g) caster sugar
2 tablespoons coffee-flavoured liqueur
3 egg whites, beaten lightly
24 coffee beans

1 Preheat oven to 180°C/160°C fan-forced. Grease oven trays; line with baking paper.
2 Dissolve coffee in the hot water in large bowl. Add almond meal, sugar, liqueur and egg whites; stir until mixture forms a firm paste.
3 Roll level tablespoons of mixture into balls; place on trays 3cm apart; flatten with hand. Press coffee beans into tops of biscuits.
4 Bake biscuits about 15 minutes. Cool biscuits on trays.

preparation time 15 minutes **cooking time** 15 minutes **makes** 24
nutritional count per biscuit 8.7g total fat (0.8g saturated fat);
606kJ (145 cal); 11.7g carbohydrate; 3.6g protein; 1.4g fibre

Yogurt, berry and white chocolate muffins

1½ cups (225g) wholemeal self-raising flour
½ cup (110g) caster sugar
2 tablespoons vegetable oil
2 eggs, beaten lightly
1 cup (280g) low-fat yogurt
1 cup (150g) frozen mixed berries
100g white eating chocolate, chopped coarsely

1 Preheat oven to 180°C/160°C fan-forced. Grease 12-hole
(⅓-cup/80ml) muffin pan.
2 Combine sifted flour and sugar in large bowl. Add remaining ingredients;
mix batter until just combined. Divide batter among pan holes.
3 Bake muffins about 30 minutes. Stand muffins 5 minutes before serving,
warm, dusted with sifted icing sugar, if you like.

preparation time 10 minutes **cooking time** 25 minutes **makes** 12
nutritional count per muffin 7.2g total fat (2.5g saturated fat);
807kJ (193 cal); 25.3g carbohydrate; 5.6g protein; 2.4g fibre

Maple-syrup butter cookies

125g butter, softened
½ teaspoon vanilla extract
⅓ cup (80ml) maple syrup
¾ cup (110g) plain flour
¼ cup (35g) cornflour

1 Preheat oven to 180°C/160°C fan-forced. Grease oven trays; line with baking paper.
2 Beat butter, extract and syrup in small bowl with electric mixer until light and fluffy; stir in combined sifted flours.
3 Spoon mixture into piping bag fitted with 1cm fluted tube. Pipe stars about 3cm apart onto trays.
4 Bake cookies about 15 minutes. Cool cookies on trays.

preparation time 20 minutes **cooking time** 15 minutes **makes** 24
nutritional count per cookie 4.3g total fat (2.8g saturated fat);
297kJ (71 cal); 7.5g carbohydrate; 0.5g protein; 0.2g fibre

Golden pecan twists

2 tablespoons golden syrup
⅓ cup (40g) finely chopped pecans
125g butter, softened
¼ teaspoon vanilla extract
⅓ cup (75g) caster sugar
1 egg yolk
1 cup (150g) plain flour

1 Preheat oven to 180°C/160°C fan-forced. Grease oven trays; line with baking paper.
2 Combine half the golden syrup with nuts in small bowl.
3 Beat butter, extract, sugar, remaining golden syrup and egg yolk in small bowl with electric mixer until light and fluffy. Stir in sifted flour.
4 Shape rounded teaspoons of mixture into balls; roll each ball into 12cm log. Twist each log into a loop, overlapping one end over the other. Place twists on trays 3cm apart; top each twist with ½ teaspoon nut mixture. Bake about 10 minutes; cool twists on trays.

preparation time 25 minutes **cooking time** 10 minutes **makes** 30
nutritional count per twist 4.6g total fat (2.4g saturated fat);
314kJ (75 cal); 7.5g carbohydrate; 0.8g protein; 0.3g fibre

Sticky pecan tarts

These tarts must be served warm to be enjoyed at their best.

3 sheets ready-rolled puff pastry
cooking-oil spray
60g butter
2 tablespoons brown sugar
2 tablespoons light corn syrup
1 tablespoon maple syrup
1 cup (120g) roasted pecans
⅓ cup (25g) shredded coconut, toasted
1 teaspoon ground nutmeg

1 Preheat oven to 220°C/200°C fan-forced. Grease 12-hole
(⅓-cup/80ml) muffin pan.
2 Cut twelve 8cm rounds from pastry. Place rounds in pan holes;
prick bases with fork, spray with cooking-oil spray. Top with another
muffin pan (to stop pastry from puffing up); bake 5 minutes. Remove
top pan; bake 2 minutes.
3 Meanwhile, combine butter, sugar and syrups in medium saucepan;
cook, stirring, without boiling, until sugar dissolves, then simmer for
5 minutes. Remove from heat; stir in nuts, coconut and nutmeg.
4 Divide pecan mixture among pastry cases; bake about 5 minutes.

preparation time 15 minutes **cooking time** 15 minutes **makes** 12
nutritional count per tart 44.9g total fat (18.9g saturated fat);
2579kJ (617 cal); 45.5g carbohydrate; 7g protein; 3.4g fibre

Chocolate chip cookies

125g butter, softened
½ teaspoon vanilla extract
⅓ cup (75g) caster sugar
⅓ cup (75g) firmly packed brown sugar
1 egg
1 cup (150g) plain flour
½ teaspoon bicarbonate of soda
150g milk eating chocolate, chopped coarsely
½ cup (50g) walnuts, chopped coarsely

1 Preheat oven to 180°C/160°C fan-forced. Grease oven trays; line with baking paper.
2 Beat butter, extract, sugars and egg in small bowl with electric mixer until smooth; do not overbeat. Transfer mixture to medium bowl; stir in sifted flour and soda then chocolate and nuts.
3 Drop level tablespoons of mixture onto trays 5cm apart.
4 Bake cookies about 15 minutes. Cool cookies on trays.

preparation time 15 minutes **cooking time** 15 minutes **makes** 24
nutritional count per cookie 7.7g total fat (4g saturated fat);
568kJ (136 cal); 14.6g carbohydrate; 1.8g protein; 0.4g fibre

Pear and almond friands

6 egg whites
185g butter, melted
1 cup (120g) almond meal
1½ cups (240g) icing sugar
¾ cup (110g) plain flour
1 small pear (180g), peeled, cored, chopped finely
¼ cup (20g) flaked almonds

1 Preheat oven to 200°C/180°C fan-forced. Grease 12-hole
(⅓-cup/80ml) muffin pan.
2 Whisk egg whites with a fork in medium bowl until frothy. Add
butter, meal, sifted icing sugar and flour, then pear; stir until combined.
3 Place ¼-cups of mixture into pan holes; sprinkle with nuts.
4 Bake friands about 20 minutes. Stand 5 minutes before turning,
top-side up, onto wire rack to cool.

preparation time 15 minutes **cooking time** 20 minutes **makes** 12
nutritional count per friand 19.2g total fat (8.8g saturated fat);
1300kJ (311 cal); 28.8g carbohydrate; 5.3g protein; 1.6g fibre

Vanilla bean thins

1 vanilla bean, halved lengthways
30g butter, softened
¼ cup (55g) caster sugar
1 egg white, beaten lightly
¼ cup (35g) plain flour

1 Preheat oven to 200°C/180°C fan-forced. Grease oven trays;
line with baking paper.
2 Scrape vanilla bean seeds into medium bowl with butter and
sugar, discard vanilla pod. Stir mixture until combined then stir in
egg white and flour.
3 Spoon mixture into piping bag fitted with 5mm plain tube. Pipe
6cm-long strips (making them slightly wider at both ends) 5cm apart
on trays.
4 Bake biscuits about 5 minutes or until edges are browned lightly.
Cool biscuits on trays.

preparation time 20 minutes **cooking time** 5 minutes **makes** 24
nutritional count per biscuit 1g total fat (0.7g saturated fat);
100kJ (24 cal); 3.4g carbohydrate; 0.3g protein; 0.1g fibre

fast
weeknights

Chicken, lentil and cauliflower pilaf

You need to buy a barbecued chicken weighing approximately 900g
to get the amount of chicken meat required for this recipe.

1 medium brown onion (150g), sliced thinly
1 clove garlic, crushed
2 tablespoons madras curry paste
1 cup (200g) basmati rice
½ small cauliflower (500g), cut into florets
400g can brown lentils, rinsed, drained
1 cup (250ml) chicken stock
1 cup (250ml) water
2 cups (320g) coarsely chopped barbecued chicken
½ cup firmly packed fresh coriander leaves

1 Cook onion and garlic in heated oiled large frying pan until onion
softens. Add paste; cook, stirring, about 5 minutes or until fragrant.
2 Add rice, cauliflower and lentils; stir to coat in onion mixture. Add stock,
the water and chicken; bring to the boil. Reduce heat; simmer, covered
tightly, about 15 minutes or until rice is tender and liquid is absorbed.
3 Remove from heat; fluff pilaf with fork. Stir in coriander; serve with lime
wedges, pappadums and chutney, if you like.

preparation time 10 minutes **cooking time** 20 minutes **serves** 4
nutritional count per serving 10.7g total fat (2.3g saturated fat);
1814kJ (434 cal); 50.2g carbohydrate; 36.6g protein; 6.1g fibre

Chicken, tomato and fetta patties with spinach salad

750g chicken mince
⅓ cup (50g) drained semi-dried tomatoes, chopped coarsely
1 egg
½ cup (35g) stale breadcrumbs
200g fetta cheese, crumbled
1 small white onion (80g), sliced thinly
100g baby spinach leaves
1 tablespoon olive oil
1 tablespoon balsamic vinegar

1 Combine mince, tomato, egg, breadcrumbs and half the cheese in large bowl; shape mixture into 12 patties.
2 Cook patties in heated oiled large frying pan, in batches, until cooked through. Drain on absorbent paper.
3 Meanwhile, combine onion, spinach, oil, vinegar and remaining cheese in medium bowl. Serve patties with spinach salad.

preparation time 20 minutes **cooking time** 10 minutes **serves** 4
nutritional count per serving 33.7g total fat (13.3g saturated fat);
2320kJ (555 cal); 11.8g carbohydrate; 50.1g protein; 3.2g fibre

Lamb cutlets niçoise

12 french-trimmed lamb cutlets (600g)
1 large cos lettuce, chopped coarsely
420g can white beans, rinsed, drained
3 medium tomatoes (450g), cut into wedges
lemon anchovy dressing
4 drained anchovy fillets, chopped finely
3 cloves garlic, crushed
3 teaspoons finely grated lemon rind
⅓ cup (80ml) lemon juice
⅓ cup (80ml) olive oil

1 Make lemon anchovy dressing.
2 Combine lamb and 2 tablespoons of the dressing in large bowl.
3 Cook lamb in heated oiled large frying pan, uncovered, in batches, until cooked as desired. Remove from heat; drizzle with 1 tablespoon of the dressing, cover to keep warm.
4 Combine remaining dressing, lettuce, beans and tomato in large bowl. Serve lamb with salad.
lemon anchovy dressing Place ingredients in screw-top jar; shake well.

preparation time 10 minutes **cooking time** 20 minutes **serves** 4
nutritional count per serving 33g total fat (8.8g saturated fat); 1852kJ (443 cal); 9.9g carbohydrate; 24.8g protein; 5.2g fibre

Pasta with capers and anchovies

375g spaghetti
2 tablespoons olive oil
3 cloves garlic, sliced thinly
¼ cup (50g) rinsed, drained baby capers
10 anchovy fillets, chopped finely
1 tablespoon finely grated lemon rind
1 tablespoon lemon juice
¼ cup coarsely chopped fresh flat-leaf parsley

1 Cook pasta in large saucepan of boiling water until tender; drain.
2 Meanwhile, heat oil in medium frying pan; cook garlic, stirring, until fragrant. Add capers and anchovies; stir gently until hot. Pour caper and anchovy mixture over pasta; stir in rind and juice. Stir in parsley just before serving.

preparation time 10 minutes **cooking time** 10 minutes **serves** 4
nutritional count per serving 11.1g total fat (1.7g saturated fat);
1781kJ (426 cal); 65.6g carbohydrate; 13.3g protein; 3.8g fibre

Almond and coriander chicken with lemon mayonnaise

1½ cups (180g) almond meal
2 teaspoons dried chilli flakes
½ cup finely chopped fresh coriander
1 tablespoon finely grated lemon rind
2 eggs
4 x 200g chicken breast fillets
⅓ cup (50g) plain flour
vegetable oil, for shallow-frying
lemon mayonnaise
⅔ cup (200g) mayonnaise
1 teaspoon finely grated lemon.rind
¼ cup (60ml) lemon juice

1 Preheat oven to 220°C/200°C fan-forced.
2 Make lemon mayonnaise.
3 Combine meal, chilli, coriander and rind in medium shallow bowl. Whisk eggs lightly in another medium shallow bowl. Coat chicken in flour, shake off excess. Dip chicken in egg then coat in almond mixture.
4 Heat oil in large frying pan; cook chicken, in batches, until browned. Place chicken on oven tray; bake, uncovered, in oven, about 10 minutes or until cooked through.
5 Slice chicken into thick pieces; serve with mayonnaise.
lemon mayonnaise Combine ingredients in small bowl.

preparation time 15 minutes **cooking time** 10 minutes **serves** 4
nutritional count per serving 81.8g total fat (11.1g saturated fat); 4402kJ (1053 cal); 21.6g carbohydrate; 57.2g protein; 5.2g fibre

Lamb teriyaki with broccolini

1 tablespoon vegetable oil
800g lamb strips
4 green onions, chopped coarsely
3cm piece fresh ginger (15g), grated
175g broccolini, chopped coarsely
150g green beans, trimmed, halved crossways
⅓ cup (80ml) teriyaki sauce
2 tablespoons honey
2 teaspoons sesame oil
1 tablespoon toasted sesame seeds

1 Heat half the vegetable oil in wok; stir-fry lamb, in batches, until browned.
2 Heat remaining vegetable oil in wok; stir-fry onion and ginger until onion softens. Add broccolini and beans; stir-fry until vegetables are tender. Remove from wok.
3 Add sauce, honey and sesame oil to wok; bring to the boil. Boil, uncovered, about 3 minutes or until sauce thickens slightly. Return lamb and vegetables to wok; stir-fry until hot. Sprinkle with seeds.

preparation time 10 minutes **cooking time** 15 minutes **serves** 4
nutritional count per serving 15.9g total fat (4.3g saturated fat); 1626kJ (389 cal); 14.1g carbohydrate; 45.7g protein; 3.4g fibre

Pumpkin and chickpea ratatouille

600g piece jap pumpkin, chopped coarsely
1 tablespoon olive oil
1 medium red onion (170g), sliced thinly
2 cloves garlic, sliced thinly
2 tablespoons tomato paste
2 tablespoons red wine vinegar
400g can crushed tomatoes
½ cup (125ml) water
1 teaspoon ground allspice
400g can chickpeas, rinsed, drained

1 Preheat oven to 220°C/200°C fan-forced.
2 Place pumpkin, in single layer, on oven tray; drizzle with half the oil. Roast, uncovered, about 20 minutes or until tender.
3 Heat remaining oil in large saucepan; cook onion and garlic, stirring, until onion softens. Add paste; cook, stirring, 1 minute. Add vinegar; cook, stirring, 1 minute. Add undrained tomatoes, the water, allspice, chickpeas and pumpkin; bring to the boil. Simmer 5 minutes.

preparation time 15 minutes **cooking time** 20 minutes **serves** 4
nutritional count per serving 6.8g total fat (1.3g saturated fat); 899kJ (215 cal); 25.3g carbohydrate; 9.1g protein; 7.4g fibre

Mixed mushroom stroganoff

375g fettuccine pasta
1 tablespoon olive oil
20g butter
3 shallots (75g), sliced thinly
2 cloves garlic, sliced thinly
3 teaspoons smoked paprika
2 tablespoons dijon mustard
350g button mushrooms, sliced thinly
200g swiss brown mushrooms, sliced thinly
200g shiitake mushrooms, sliced thinly
¼ cup (60ml) dry white wine
¾ cup (180ml) vegetable stock
1 cup (240g) sour cream

1 Cook pasta in large saucepan of boiling water until tender; drain. Rinse under cold water, drain.
2 Meanwhile, heat oil and half the butter in large saucepan, add shallot and garlic; cook, stirring, until shallot softens. Add paprika and mustard; cook, stirring, 1 minute. Stir in mushrooms and remaining butter. Cover; cook 10 minutes, stirring occasionally.
3 Add wine and stock to pan; cook, uncovered, about 5 minutes or until liquid is reduced slightly. Add sour cream; simmer gently, uncovered, 5 minutes. Serve over pasta.

preparation time 15 minutes **cooking time** 25 minutes **serves** 4
nutritional count per serving 34.4g total fat (19.3g saturated fat); 2863kJ (685 cal); 68.7g carbohydrate; 18.8g protein; 8.3g fibre

Pork larb with broccolini

1 tablespoon peanut oil
2 cloves garlic, crushed
600g pork mince
⅓ cup (90g) grated palm sugar
2 tablespoons fish sauce
4 kaffir lime leaves, sliced finely
½ cup (40g) fried shallots
⅓ cup (45g) roasted unsalted peanuts
350g broccolini, trimmed, halved lengthways
1 tablespoon lime juice
1 cup loosely packed fresh coriander leaves
1 fresh long red chilli, sliced thinly
2 tablespoons coarsely chopped roasted unsalted peanuts

1 Heat oil in wok; stir-fry garlic and mince until mince is cooked through.
Remove from wok with slotted spoon.
2 Add sugar, sauce, lime leaves, shallots and nuts to wok; bring to the
boil. Reduce heat; simmer, uncovered, 1 minute. Return pork to wok;
cook, uncovered, about 2 minutes or until larb mixture is slightly dry
and sticky.
3 Meanwhile, boil, steam or microwave broccolini until tender; drain.
4 Stir juice and three-quarters of the coriander into larb off the heat;
serve tossed with broccolini and sprinkled with remaining coriander,
chilli and coarsely chopped nuts.

preparation time 15 minutes **cooking time** 10 minutes **serves** 4
nutritional count per serving 23.9g total fat (6g saturated fat);
2006kJ (480 cal); 25g carbohydrate; 39.5g protein; 5.5g fibre

Chicken sang choy bow

Remove eight large outer leaves from the trimmed wombok before shredding it.

100g rice stick noodles
2 teaspoons vegetable oil
500g chicken mince
1 medium red onion (170g), chopped finely
1 tablespoon curry powder
1 large carrot (180g), chopped finely
2 tablespoons oyster sauce
2 tablespoons char siu sauce
½ small wombok (350g), shredded coarsely
100g snow peas, sliced lengthways
8 large wombok leaves

1 Place noodles in medium heatproof bowl, cover with boiling water; stand 3 minutes, drain. Cut into random lengths.
2 Heat oil in wok; stir-fry mince and onion until mince changes colour. Add curry powder; stir-fry until fragrant. Add carrot; stir-fry until carrot softens.
3 Add sauces, wombok and peas to wok; stir-fry about 2 minutes or until vegetables soften.
4 Divide wombok leaves among serving bowls. Toss noodles with mince mixture; divide among wombok cups.

preparation time 10 minutes **cooking time** 10 minutes **serves** 4
nutritional count per serving 13.7g total fat (3.4g saturated fat); 1572kJ (376 cal); 29.9g carbohydrate; 29.7g protein; 6.3g fibre

Chorizo and white bean braise

You need about 1kg of untrimmed silver beet to get the amount needed for this recipe.

4 chorizo sausages (680g), sliced thickly
2 cloves garlic, sliced thinly
2 baby fennel bulbs (260g), trimmed, chopped coarsely
400g can chopped tomatoes
⅓ cup (80ml) chicken stock
2 x 420g cans white beans, rinsed, drained
1 cup (250ml) water
250g trimmed silver beet, chopped coarsely

1 Preheat oven to 200°C/180°C fan-forced.
2 Cook chorizo in heated large flameproof dish, stirring, about 5 minutes. Add garlic and fennel; cook, stirring, 2 minutes.
3 Add undrained tomatoes, stock, beans and the water; cook, uncovered, in oven, 15 minutes. Stir in silver beet; cook, uncovered, about 5 minutes or until silver beet wilts.

preparation time 10 minutes **cooking time** 25 minutes **serves** 4
nutritional count per serving 52g total fat (18.6g saturated fat); 3214kJ (769 cal); 24.8g carbohydrate; 44.2g protein; 14g fibre

Asian-style fried egg with mushrooms

¼ cup (60ml) oyster sauce
1 tablespoon light soy sauce
2 teaspoons brown sugar
1 tablespoon peanut oil
1 small red onion (100g), sliced thinly
2 cloves garlic, sliced thinly
200g swiss brown mushrooms, sliced thickly
150g oyster mushrooms, sliced thickly
100g shiitake mushrooms, sliced thickly
peanut oil, for deep-frying
4 eggs

1 Combine sauces and sugar in small bowl.
2 Heat oil in wok; stir-fry onion and garlic until onion softens. Add mushrooms; stir-fry 5 minutes. Add half the sauce mixture; stir-fry 5 minutes. Remove mushrooms from wok.
3 Meanwhile, heat oil over high heat in medium saucepan. Add one egg; fry 30 seconds. Turn egg with slotted spoon; fry 30 seconds. Drain egg on absorbent paper. Repeat with remaining eggs.
4 Serve mushrooms topped with egg; drizzle with remaining sauce mixture.

preparation time 15 minutes **cooking time** 20 minutes **serves** 4
nutritional count per serving 14.5g total fat (3.2g saturated fat);
903kJ (216 cal); 7.9g carbohydrate; 11.7g protein; 4.6g fibre

Tofu, cashew and vegie stir-fry

We used cryovac-packed ready-to-serve sweet chilli tofu, available from many supermarkets and Asian food stores. Packaged fresh stir-fry vegies are available from supermarkets.

1 tablespoon vegetable oil
1 fresh long red chilli, sliced thinly
500g packaged fresh stir-fry vegetables
400g packaged marinated tofu pieces, chopped coarsely
½ cup (75g) roasted unsalted cashews
⅓ cup (80ml) hoisin sauce
1 tablespoon lime juice

1 Heat oil in wok; stir-fry chilli, vegetables, tofu and nuts until vegetables are just tender.
2 Add sauce and juice to wok; stir-fry until hot.

preparation time 5 minutes **cooking time** 10 minutes **serves** 4
nutritional count per serving 22.6g total fat (3.4g saturated fat); 1563kJ (374 cal); 20.9g carbohydrate; 18.2g protein; 8.4g fibre

Cheesy-vegie pasta bake

375g penne pasta
300g broccoli, cut into florets
500g cauliflower, cut into florets
2 teaspoons vegetable oil
1 large brown onion (200g), chopped finely
1 teaspoon mustard powder
1 teaspoon sweet paprika
¼ cup (35g) plain flour
1½ cups (375ml) low-fat milk
420g can tomato soup
400g can diced tomatoes
1½ cups (180g) coarsely grated reduced-fat cheddar cheese
2 tablespoons finely chopped fresh flat-leaf parsley

1 Cook pasta in large saucepan of boiling water, uncovered, until just tender; drain. Cover to keep warm.
2 Meanwhile, cook broccoli and cauliflower in medium saucepan of boiling water, uncovered, until tender; drain. Cover to keep warm.
3 Preheat grill.
4 Heat oil in same large pan; cook onion, stirring, until softened. Add mustard, paprika and flour; cook, stirring, over low heat, 2 minutes. Gradually stir in milk and soup; stir over heat until mixture boils and thickens. Add undrained tomatoes; cook, stirring, until mixture is hot.
5 Stir pasta, broccoli, cauliflower and 1 cup of the cheese into tomato mixture. Divide pasta mixture among six 1-cup (250ml) flameproof dishes, sprinkle with remaining cheese; grill until cheese melts and is browned lightly. Sprinkle pasta bake with parsley just before serving.

preparation time 15 minutes **cooking time** 20 minutes **serves** 6
nutritional count per serving 10.9g total fat (5.4g saturated fat); 1952kJ (467 cal); 62.3g carbohydrate; 25.5g protein; 7.4g fibre

Chilli fried rice with chicken and broccolini

You need to cook 1 cup (200g) white long-grain rice the day before making this recipe. Spread evenly onto a tray; refrigerate overnight. You need a large barbecued chicken, weighing approximately 900g, for this recipe.

1 tablespoon peanut oil
3 eggs, beaten lightly
1 medium brown onion (150g), sliced thinly
1 clove garlic, crushed
2 fresh long red chillies, sliced thinly
175g broccolini, chopped coarsely
2 cups (320g) shredded barbecued chicken
3 cups cooked white long-grain rice
1 tablespoon light soy sauce
1 tablespoon hoisin sauce

1 Heat about a third of the oil in wok; add half the egg, swirl wok to make a thin omelette. Remove omelette from wok; roll then cut into thin strips. Repeat process using another third of the oil and remaining egg.
2 Heat remaining oil in wok; stir-fry onion, garlic and chilli until onion softens. Add broccolini; stir-fry until tender.
3 Add remaining ingredients to wok; stir-fry until hot. Add omelette; toss gently.

preparation time 10 minutes **cooking time** 15 minutes **serves** 4
nutritional count per serving 15.3g total fat (3.8g saturated fat); 1881kJ (450 cal); 44.6g carbohydrate; 30.9g protein; 4.1g fibre

Tuna and chilli pasta

375g angel hair pasta
425g can tuna in oil
4 cloves garlic, sliced thinly
1 teaspoon dried chilli flakes
⅓ cup (80ml) dry white wine
400g can chopped tomatoes
1 tablespoon lemon juice

1 Cook pasta in large saucepan of boiling water until tender; drain, reserving ¼ cup cooking liquid. Rinse pasta under cold water, drain.
2 Meanwhile, drain tuna, reserving 2 tablespoons of the oil. Heat oil in medium frying pan, add garlic; cook, stirring, until fragrant. Add chilli and wine; cook, uncovered, until wine is almost evaporated.
3 Add undrained tomatoes, tuna and reserved cooking liquid to wok; simmer until liquid has reduced slightly. Remove from heat; stir in juice. Combine pasta and sauce in large bowl.

preparation time 5 minutes **cooking time** 10 minutes **serves** 4
nutritional count per serving 22.3g total fat (3.2g saturated fat); 2617kJ (626 cal); 67.5g carbohydrate; 32.5g protein; 4.8g fibre

Pumpkin and sage ravioli

¼ cup (40g) pine nuts
2 teaspoons olive oil
3 cloves garlic, crushed
600g piece pumpkin, cut into 1cm pieces
625g ricotta ravioli
300ml cream
¼ cup (20g) finely grated parmesan cheese
2 tablespoons coarsely chopped fresh sage
2 tablespoons lemon juice

1 Cook nuts in large frying pan, stirring, until browned lightly; remove from pan.
2 Heat oil in same pan; cook garlic and pumpkin, covered, stirring occasionally, about 10 minutes or until pumpkin is almost tender.
3 Meanwhile, cook ravioli in large saucepan of boiling water, uncovered, until just tender; drain.
4 Add nuts, cream, cheese and sage to pumpkin mixture; bring to the boil. Reduce heat; simmer, uncovered, 5 minutes. Add ravioli and juice; stir until hot.

preparation time 10 minutes **cooking time** 15 minutes **serves** 4
nutritional count per serving 51.7g total fat (26.7g saturated fat);
2826kJ (676 cal); 32.5g carbohydrate; 19.2g protein; 4.7g fibre

Hokkien chilli beef

¼ cup (60ml) sweet chilli sauce
2 tablespoons plum sauce
600g piece beef rump steak, sliced thinly
450g hokkien noodles
1 tablespoon peanut oil
4 green onions, cut into 2cm lengths
1 clove garlic, crushed
1 medium red capsicum (200g), sliced thinly
115g baby corn, halved lengthways
150g sugar snap peas, trimmed
½ cup (125ml) vegetable stock

1 Combine sauces with beef in medium bowl.
2 Place noodles in medium heatproof bowl, cover with boiling water; separate with fork, drain.
3 Heat oil in wok; stir-fry beef mixture, in batches, until browned.
4 Add onion and garlic to wok; stir-fry until onion browns. Add capsicum and corn to wok; stir-fry until vegetables are almost softened. Return beef to wok with noodles, peas and stock; stir-fry until hot.

preparation time 15 minutes **cooking time** 15 minutes **serves** 4
nutritional count per serving 17g total fat (5.7g saturated);
2771kJ (663 cal); 75.7g carbohydrate; 47.9g protein; 5.9g fibre

Chicken and yellow bean relish

Due to the richness of this relish, you only need to serve a small amount to enjoy its delicious flavour.

3 cloves garlic, quartered
2 purple shallots (50g), chopped coarsely
1 tablespoon vegetable oil
2 tablespoons yellow bean paste
150g chicken mince
⅓ cup (80ml) coconut cream
2 tablespoons chicken stock
¼ teaspoon dried chilli flakes
⅓ cup loosely packed fresh coriander leaves
⅓ cup coarsely chopped fresh mint
8 large trimmed wombok leaves

1 Using mortar and pestle, crush garlic and shallot until mixture forms a paste.
2 Heat oil in wok; stir-fry garlic mixture until browned lightly. Add yellow bean paste; stir-fry until fragrant.
3 Add mince to wok; stir-fry until cooked through. Add coconut cream, stock and chilli; bring to the boil. Reduce heat; simmer, uncovered, about 5 minutes or until thickened. Remove from heat; stir in herbs.
4 Serve relish with wombok leaves, and sliced cucumber and carrot sticks, if you like.

preparation time 10 minutes **cooking time** 10 minutes **makes** 1 cup
nutritional count per tablespoon 4.1g total fat (1.7g saturated); 238kJ (57 cal); 1.4g carbohydrate; 3.4g protein; 1g fibre

Beef kway teow

¼ cup (60ml) oyster sauce
2 tablespoons kecap manis
2 tablespoons chinese cooking wine
1 teaspoon sambal oelek
3 cloves garlic, crushed
2cm piece fresh ginger (10g), grated
2 tablespoons peanut oil
500g beef strips
450g fresh wide rice noodles
6 green onions, cut into 2cm lengths
1 small red capsicum (150g), sliced thinly
1 small green capsicum (150g), sliced thinly
¼ cup coarsely chopped garlic chives
2 cups (160g) bean sprouts

1 Combine sauces, cooking wine, sambal, garlic and ginger in small jug.
2 Heat half the oil in wok; stir-fry beef, in batches, until browned lightly.
3 Place noodles in large heatproof bowl, cover with boiling water;
separate with fork, drain.
4 Heat remaining oil in wok; stir-fry onion and capsicums until tender.
5 Return beef to wok with sauce mixture, noodles, chives and sprouts;
stir-fry until hot.

preparation time 10 minutes **cooking time** 10 minutes **serves** 4
nutritional count per serving 17.7g total fat (4.8g saturated fat);
2195kJ (525 cal); 53g carbohydrate; 34.4g protein; 3.8g fibre

Spaghetti carbonara with peas

4 egg yolks
¾ cup (60g) finely grated parmesan cheese
4 rindless bacon rashers (260g), chopped finely
2 cloves garlic, sliced thinly
1 cup (120g) frozen peas
375g spaghetti

1 Combine egg yolks and cheese in small bowl.
2 Cook bacon over heat in medium frying pan about 5 minutes or until starting to crisp. Add garlic; cook, stirring, 1 minute. Add peas; cook, stirring, until heated through.
3 Meanwhile, cook pasta in large saucepan of boiling water until tender; drain, reserving ¼ cup cooking liquid.
4 Return pasta to pan. Add bacon mixture, egg mixture and reserved cooking liquid to pasta; stir over heat about 1 minute.
5 Serve with extra parmesan cheese, if you like.

preparation time 15 minutes **cooking time** 10 minutes **serves** 4
nutritional count per serving 15.3g total fat (6.3g saturated fat); 2332kJ (558 cal); 66.8g carbohydrate; 35g protein; 5.1g fibre

Ravioli with tomato, pea and basil sauce

2 teaspoons olive oil
6 slices pancetta (90g)
1 clove garlic, crushed
700g bottled tomato pasta sauce
¼ cup (60ml) dry white wine
2 tablespoons finely chopped fresh basil
1 cup (120g) frozen peas
625g spinach and ricotta ravioli

1 Heat oil in large frying pan; cook pancetta until crisp. Drain on absorbent paper; break into pieces.
2 Cook garlic in same pan, stirring, 1 minute. Add sauce, wine and basil; bring to the boil. Add peas, reduce heat; simmer, uncovered, 15 minutes.
3 Meanwhile, cook ravioli in large saucepan of boiling water until just tender; drain. Return ravioli to pan, add sauce; toss to combine. Divide among serving bowls; top with pancetta.

preparation time 10 minutes **cooking time** 15 minutes **serves** 4
nutritional count per serving 12.8g total fat (4.1g saturated fat); 1593kJ (381 cal); 46.6g carbohydrate; 20.1g protein; 7.4g fibre

Pad thai

540g uncooked medium king prawns
¼ cup (85g) tamarind concentrate
⅓ cup (80ml) sweet chilli sauce
2 tablespoons fish sauce
⅓ cup firmly packed fresh coriander leaves
¼ cup (35g) roasted unsalted peanuts
¼ cup (20g) fried shallots
2 cups (160g) bean sprouts
4 green onions, sliced thinly
375g dried rice stick noodles
1 tablespoon peanut oil
2 cloves garlic, crushed
4cm piece fresh ginger (20g), grated
3 fresh small red thai chillies, chopped finely
250g pork mince
2 eggs, beaten lightly
1 lime, quartered

1 Shell and devein prawns, leaving tails intact.
2 Combine tamarind and sauces in small jug.
3 Combine coriander, nuts, shallots, half the sprouts and half the onion in medium bowl.
4 Place noodles in large heatproof bowl, cover with boiling water; stand until just tender, drain.
5 Meanwhile, heat oil in wok; stir-fry garlic, ginger and chilli until fragrant. Add mince; stir-fry until cooked. Add prawns; stir-fry 1 minute. Add egg; stir-fry until set. Add tamarind mixture, remaining sprouts and onion, and noodles; stir-fry until combined.
6 Divide mixture among serving bowls; sprinkle with coriander mixture, serve with lime wedges.

preparation time 25 minutes **cooking time** 10 minutes **serves** 4
nutritional count per serving 17.5g total fat (3.9g saturated fat);
1827kJ (437 cal); 30.3g carbohydrate; 36.8g protein; 4.9g fibre

Pork fried rice

You need to cook about 1⅓ cups (265g) brown long-grain rice the day before making this recipe. Spread evenly onto a tray; refrigerate overnight.

3 teaspoons peanut oil
2 eggs, beaten lightly
1 medium brown onion (150g), sliced thinly
1 clove garlic, crushed
2 rindless rashers bacon (130g), sliced thinly
200g pork fillet, sliced thinly
150g button mushrooms, quartered
150g sugar snap peas, trimmed, halved crossways
1 medium carrot (120g), chopped finely
3 cups cold cooked brown long-grain rice
2 tablespoons kecap manis
4 green onions, sliced thinly

1 Heat one teaspoon of the oil in wok, add half the egg; swirl wok to make a thin omelette. Remove omelette from wok; roll then cut into thin strips. Repeat process using another teaspoon of oil and remaining egg.
2 Heat remaining oil in wok; stir-fry onion and garlic until onion softens. Add bacon and pork; stir-fry until bacon is crisp. Add mushrooms, peas and carrot; stir-fry about 3 minutes or until carrot is just tender.
3 Add rice and kecap to wok; stir-fry until hot. Toss omelette and onion through fried rice just before serving.

preparation time 15 minutes **cooking time** 20 minutes **serves** 4
nutritional count per serving 13g total fat (3.7g saturated fat);
1726kJ (413 cal); 42.8g carbohydrate; 28.2g protein; 5.2g fibre

Ginger-plum chicken and noodle stir-fry

We used a 400g packet of prepared asian stir-fry vegetables for this recipe, available from supermarkets.

2 tablespoons vegetable oil
600g chicken breast fillets, sliced thinly
450g hokkien noodles
1 medium brown onion (150g), sliced thinly
1 clove garlic, crushed
3cm piece fresh ginger (15g), grated
400g packaged fresh asian stir-fry vegetables
2 tablespoons sweet chilli sauce
2 tablespoons plum sauce

1 Heat half the oil in wok; stir-fry chicken, in batches, until browned.
2 Meanwhile, place noodles in medium heatproof bowl, cover with boiling water; separate with fork, drain.
3 Heat remaining oil in wok; stir-fry onion, garlic and ginger until onion softens. Add vegetables; stir-fry until just tender. Return chicken to wok with noodles and sauces; stir-fry until hot.

preparation time 10 minutes **cooking time** 15 minutes **serves** 4
nutritional count per serving 19.4g total fat (4.6g saturated fat); 2784kJ (666 cal); 73.3g carbohydrate; 45.6g protein; 6.2g fibre

Spicy veal pizzaiola

2 tablespoons olive oil
2 cloves garlic, crushed
4 slices pancetta (60g), chopped finely
¼ cup (60ml) dry white wine
700g bottled tomato pasta sauce
1 teaspoon dried chilli flakes
4 x 170g veal cutlets
75g baby spinach leaves

1 Heat 2 teaspoons of the oil in large saucepan; cook garlic and pancetta, stirring, about 5 minutes. Add wine; cook, stirring, until wine is reduced by half. Add sauce and chilli; simmer, uncovered, about 15 minutes or until sauce thickens.
2 Meanwhile, heat remaining oil in large frying pan. Cook veal, uncovered, until cooked as desired.
3 Remove sauce from heat; stir in spinach. Top veal with sauce; accompany with fettuccine pasta, if you like.

preparation time 10 minutes **cooking time** 20 minutes **serves** 4
nutritional count per serving 14.6g total fat (2.8g saturated fat); 1555kJ (372 cal); 18.8g carbohydrate; 36.3g protein; 4.3g fibre

Char siu pork, corn and choy sum

2 tablespoons peanut oil
600g pork fillets, sliced thinly
2 medium brown onions (300g), cut into thin wedges
230g baby corn
300g choy sum, trimmed, chopped coarsely
2 tablespoons char siu sauce
2 teaspoons light soy sauce
2 teaspoons lime juice
1 fresh long red chilli, sliced thinly

1 Heat half the oil in wok; stir-fry pork, in batches, until browned and cooked through.
2 Heat remaining oil in wok; stir-fry onion and corn until onion softens.
3 Return pork to wok with choy sum, sauces and juice; stir-fry until hot. Sprinkle with chilli.

preparation time 10 minutes **cooking time** 15 minutes **serves** 4
nutritional count per serving 14g total fat (3g saturated fat); 1513kJ (362 cal); 18.4g carbohydrate; 37.5g protein; 5.7g fibre

Red curry lentils

1 tablespoon olive oil
1 medium brown onion (150g), quartered
2 tablespoons red curry paste
2 x 400g cans brown lentils, rinsed, drained
1 cup (250ml) vegetable stock
200g green beans, halved
2 tablespoons lime juice
⅔ cup (190g) yogurt

1 Heat oil in medium saucepan; cook onion, stirring, until soft. Add paste; cook, stirring, until fragrant. Add lentils and stock; bring to the boil. Reduce heat; simmer, uncovered, about 10 minutes or until stock has thickened. Add beans, simmer 2 minutes. Remove from heat; stir in juice.
2 Divide curry among serving bowls; serve topped with yogurt.

preparation time 5 minutes **cooking time** 15 minutes **serves** 4
nutritional count per serving 10.5g total fat (2.2g saturated fat);
865kJ (207 cal); 14.3g carbohydrate; 11g protein; 6g fibre

Lemon, pea and ricotta pasta

375g angel hair pasta
2 cups (240g) frozen peas
2 tablespoons olive oil
2 cloves garlic, sliced thinly
2 teaspoons finely grated lemon rind
½ cup (125ml) lemon juice
¾ cup (180g) ricotta cheese, crumbled

1 Cook pasta in large saucepan of boiling water until tender; add peas during last minute of pasta cooking time. Drain, reserving ¼ cup cooking liquid. Rinse pasta and peas under cold water; drain.
2 Meanwhile, heat oil in small frying pan; cook garlic, stirring, until fragrant.
3 Combine pasta and peas in large bowl with reserved cooking liquid, garlic, rind and juice; stir in cheese.

preparation time 5 minutes **cooking time** 10 minutes **serves** 4
nutritional count per serving 15.6g total fat (4.7g saturated fat); 2123kJ (508 cal); 69g carbohydrate; 19g protein; 6.9g fibre

Javanese stir-fried pork and rice noodles

450g fresh wide rice noodles
1 tablespoon vegetable oil
500g pork mince
2 cloves garlic, crushed
1 tablespoon sambal oelek
4 green onions, sliced thinly
⅓ cup (80ml) kecap manis
2 baby buk choy (300g), leaves separated
1 cup loosely packed fresh coriander leaves

1 Place noodles in large heatproof bowl, cover with boiling water; separate with fork, drain.
2 Heat oil in wok; stir-fry mince until browned. Add garlic, sambal, onion and 1 tablespoon of the kecap manis; stir-fry 1 minute.
3 Add noodles, remaining kecap manis and buk choy to wok; stir-fry until hot. Sprinkle with coriander.

preparation time 10 minutes **cooking time** 15 minutes **serves** 4
nutritional count per serving 14.5g total fat (3.8g saturated fat); 1927kJ (461 cal); 49g carbohydrate; 31.1g protein; 2.8g fibre

Rice pudding with cardamom and raisins

1 litre (4 cups) milk
300ml cream
1 cup (200g) arborio rice
½ cup (110g) caster sugar
½ teaspoon ground cardamom
½ teaspoon ground cinnamon
¾ cup (110g) raisins
caramelised apples
40g butter
¼ cup (55g) firmly packed brown sugar
2 medium apples (300g), peeled, cored, quartered

1 Combine milk, cream, rice and sugar in large saucepan; stir over heat, without boiling, until sugar dissolves. Bring to the boil; reduce heat. Cook, stirring, about 20 minutes or until rice is tender.
2 Meanwhile, make caramelised apples.
3 Stir spices and raisins into rice; cook, stirring, 5 minutes.
4 Serve rice pudding topped with apples.
caramelised apples Melt butter in small saucepan; stir in sugar and apples. Stir over low heat about 10 minutes or until sauce is thickened and apples are tender.

preparation time 5 minutes **cooking time** 25 minutes **serves** 4
nutritional count per serving 51g total fat (33.4g saturated fat);
4193kJ (1003 cal); 120g carbohydrate; 14.1g protein; 2.7g fibre

Pears with choc-mint sauce

200g peppermint cream dark chocolate, chopped coarsely
¼ cup (60ml) cream
825g can pear halves in natural juice, drained
1 litre vanilla ice-cream
4 mint slice biscuits (60g), chopped finely

1 Melt chocolate with cream in medium heatproof bowl set over medium saucepan of simmering water.
2 Divide pears among serving dishes; top with ice-cream, drizzle with sauce then sprinkle with biscuits.

preparation time 5 minutes **cooking time** 5 minutes **serves** 4
nutritional count per serving 39.9g total fat (25.2g saturated fat); 2976kJ (712 cal); 77.9g carbohydrate; 9.3g protein; 2.7g fibre

Butterscotch nougat bananas

40g butter
¼ cup (55g) brown sugar
4 small bananas (520g), cut into thirds
½ cup (125ml) thickened cream
2 tablespoons vanilla yogurt
50g nougat, chopped finely
¼ cup (35g) slivered almonds, roasted

1 Melt butter with sugar in large frying pan. Add bananas; cook, over low heat, about 5 minutes, turning occasionally, until caramelised.
2 Meanwhile, beat cream in small bowl with electric mixer until soft peaks form; fold in yogurt and nougat.
3 Serve bananas topped with nougat cream; sprinkle with nuts.

preparation time 10 minutes **cooking time** 5 minutes **serves** 4
nutritional count per serving 26.2g total fat (13.7g saturated fat);
1793kJ (429 cal); 42.4g carbohydrate; 5.1g protein; 2.8g fibre

Lemon and mixed berry self-saucing pudding

¾ cup (110g) self-raising flour
½ cup (110g) caster sugar
½ cup (125ml) skim milk
1 tablespoon finely grated lemon rind
30g butter, melted
⅓ cup (55g) icing sugar
⅔ cup (160ml) boiling water
mixed berry sauce
1 cup (150g) frozen mixed berries
1 tablespoon caster sugar
1 tablespoon water

1 Grease four deep 1¼-cup (310ml) microwave-proof dishes.
2 Make mixed berry sauce.
3 Sift flour into medium bowl, add sugar, milk, rind and butter; whisk until batter is smooth.
4 Divide berry sauce among dishes then top with batter; dust with sifted icing sugar. Carefully pour hot water over puddings. Microwave, uncovered, on MEDIUM (55%) about 10 minutes.
mixed berry sauce Combine ingredients in small saucepan; bring to the boil. Boil, uncovered, 1 minute. Remove from heat.

preparation time 15 minutes **cooking time** 15 minutes **serves** 4
nutritional count per serving 6.6g total fat (4.2g saturated fat);
1505kJ (360 cal); 68.4g carbohydrate; 4.8g protein; 2g fibre

Banana caramel sundae

70g dark eating chocolate, chopped finely
⅔ cup (70g) roasted walnuts, chopped coarsely
1 litre vanilla ice-cream
4 medium bananas (800g), chopped coarsely
caramel sauce
100g butter
½ cup (125ml) cream
½ cup (110g) firmly packed brown sugar

1 Make caramel sauce.
2 Divide one-third of the sauce among six ¾-cup (180ml) glasses; layer glasses with half the chocolate, nuts, ice-cream and banana. Repeat layering process, ending with a layer of the sauce.
caramel sauce Stir ingredients in small saucepan over low heat until sugar dissolves; bring to the boil. Reduce heat; simmer, uncovered, 5 minutes. Cool 15 minutes.

preparation time 10 minutes **cooking time** 10 minutes **serves** 6
nutritional count per serving 41.7g total fat (22.4g saturated fat); 2579kJ (617 cal); 56.1g carbohydrate; 6.9g protein; 2.4g fibre

Berry hazelnut crumbles

2 cups (300g) frozen mixed berries
1 tablespoon lemon juice
2 tablespoons brown sugar
½ cup (60g) finely chopped roasted hazelnuts
2 tablespoons plain flour
20g cold butter
¼ cup (20g) rolled oats

1 Preheat oven to 220°C/200°C fan-forced. Grease four shallow
¾-cup (180ml) ovenproof dishes; place on oven tray.
2 Combine berries, juice, half the sugar and half the nuts in medium
bowl; divide mixture among dishes.
3 Blend or process remaining sugar and nuts with flour and butter until
ingredients come together; stir in oats. Sprinkle over berry mixture.
4 Bake crumbles, uncovered, about 20 minutes or until browned lightly.
Serve with custard, if you like.

preparation time 10 minutes **cooking time** 20 minutes **serves** 4
nutritional count per serving 14.6g total fat (3.2g saturated fat);
915kJ (219 cal); 16.8g carbohydrate; 4.8g protein; 3.9g fibre

fast
weekends

Chilli, salt and pepper seafood

500g uncooked medium king prawns
300g cleaned squid hoods
300g scallops, roe removed
2 teaspoons sea salt
½ teaspoon cracked black pepper
½ teaspoon five-spice powder
2 fresh small red thai chillies, chopped finely
2 tablespoons peanut oil
150g sugar snap peas, trimmed
2 tablespoons light soy sauce
1 lime, cut into wedges

1 Shell and devein prawns, leaving tails intact. Cut squid down centre to open out; score inside in diagonal pattern then cut into thick strips.
2 Combine seafood, salt, pepper, five-spice and chilli in large bowl.
3 Heat half the oil in wok; stir-fry seafood, in batches, until cooked.
4 Heat remaining oil in wok; stir-fry peas until tender. Return seafood to wok with sauce; stir-fry until hot. Serve seafood with lime.

preparation time 15 minutes **cooking time** 15 minutes **serves** 4
nutritional count per serving 11g total fat (2.2g saturated fat);
1070kJ (256 cal); 2.7g carbohydrate; 35.8g protein; 1.2g fibre

Black olive tapenade

2 cups (240g) seeded black olives
1 drained anchovy fillet, rinsed
1 tablespoon drained capers, rinsed
2 teaspoons dijon mustard
2 tablespoons olive oil

1 Rinse and drain olives on absorbent paper. Blend or process olives with anchovy, capers and mustard until smooth.
2 With motor operating, add oil in a thin steady stream, processing until tapenade is smooth.
3 Serve tapenade with toasted turkish bread cut into fingers, if you like.

preparation time 5 minutes **makes** 1 cup
nutritional count per tablespoon 3.3g total fat (0.5g saturated fat); 213kJ (51 cal); 4.6g carbohydrate; 0.6g protein; 0.3g fibre

Zucchini and sumac fritters with tomato and mint salad

6 medium zucchini (700g), grated coarsely
1 medium brown onion (150g), chopped finely
1¼ cups (85g) stale breadcrumbs
3 eggs
2 tablespoons finely chopped fresh oregano
1 teaspoon sumac
2 tablespoons olive oil
3 medium tomatoes (450g), seeded, chopped finely
¼ cup coarsely chopped fresh mint
½ cup (140g) yogurt

1 Squeeze excess liquid from zucchini using absorbent paper until as dry as possible. Combine zucchini in medium bowl with onion, breadcrumbs, eggs, oregano and sumac.
2 Heat oil in large frying pan; drop rounded tablespoons of zucchini mixture, in batches, into pan. Cook until browned both sides and cooked through.
3 Meanwhile, combine tomato and mint in small bowl; serve fritters with tomato and mint salad, accompanied by yogurt.

preparation time 25 minutes **cooking time** 10 minutes **serves** 4
nutritional count per serving 15.6g total fat (3.4g saturated fat);
1208kJ (289 cal); 21.7g carbohydrate; 12.8g protein; 5g fibre

Chilli squid salad

3 cleaned squid hoods (450g)
1 tablespoon sweet chilli sauce
2 teaspoons fish sauce
2 teaspoons lime juice
1 tablespoon peanut oil
1 telegraph cucumber (400g), halved lengthways, sliced thinly
3 green onions, sliced thinly
1 cup (80g) bean sprouts
¼ cup firmly packed fresh coriander leaves
⅓ cup firmly packed fresh mint leaves
1 fresh long red chilli, sliced thinly
¼ cup (60ml) sweet chilli sauce, extra
1 tablespoon lime juice, extra

1 Cut squid hoods in half lengthways; score inside in a diagonal pattern. Cut each half into four pieces.
2 Combine squid, sauces and juice in medium bowl.
3 Heat oil in wok; stir-fry squid, in batches, until cooked through. Combine squid in large bowl with remaining ingredients.

preparation time 15 minutes **cooking time** 10 minutes **serves** 4
nutritional count per serving 6.6g total fat (1.4g saturated fat); 744kJ (178 cal); 6.5g carbohydrate; 21.4g protein; 3g fibre

Pan-fried fish with fennel salad

4 x 200g firm white fish fillets, skin-on
2 medium red capsicums (400g), chopped coarsely
2 small fennel bulbs (400g), trimmed, sliced thinly
½ cup (60g) seeded black olives
⅓ cup coarsely chopped fresh basil
2 tablespoons olive oil
1 tablespoon balsamic vinegar

1 Cook fish, skin-side down, in heated oiled large frying pan, turning once, until cooked.
2 Meanwhile, combine remaining ingredients in medium bowl. Serve fish with salad.

preparation time 10 minutes **cooking time** 10 minutes **serves** 4
nutritional count per serving 13.9g total fat (2.7g saturated fat); 1409kJ (337 cal); 8.6g carbohydrate; 42.9g protein; 2.8g fibre
tip We used blue-eye fillets in this recipe, but any firm white fish fillet can be used.

Mussels in black bean sauce

2kg medium black mussels
1 tablespoon peanut oil
6cm piece fresh ginger (30g), sliced thinly
4 cloves garlic, sliced thinly
8 green onions, sliced thinly
4 fresh small red thai chillies, chopped finely
⅓ cup (100g) black bean sauce
¼ cup (60ml) fish stock
¼ cup (60ml) water
1 cup firmly packed fresh coriander leaves

1 Scrub mussels under cold water; remove beards.
2 Heat oil in wok; stir-fry ginger, garlic, onion and chilli until fragrant. Add sauce, stock and the water; bring to the boil.
3 Add mussels; simmer, covered, about 5 minutes or until mussels open (discard any that do not). Remove from heat; sprinkle with coriander.

preparation time 10 minutes **cooking time** 10 minutes **serves** 4
nutritional count per serving 8.4g total fat (1g saturated fat); 882kJ (211 cal); 9.4g carbohydrate; 23.2g protein; 2.1g fibre

Chilli-garlic mince with snake beans

2 cloves garlic, quartered
2 long green chillies, chopped coarsely
2 fresh small red thai chillies, chopped coarsely
1 tablespoon peanut oil
600g beef mince
150g snake beans, chopped coarsely
1 medium red capsicum (200g), sliced thinly
2 tablespoons kecap asin
¼ cup (60ml) hoisin sauce
4 green onions, sliced thickly
2 tablespoons crushed peanuts

1 Blend or process garlic and chilli until mixture is finely chopped.
2 Heat half the oil in wok; stir-fry garlic mixture until fragrant. Add mince; stir-fry, in batches, until cooked through.
3 Heat remaining oil in cleaned wok; stir-fry beans and capsicum until tender.
4 Return beef to wok with sauces and onion; stir-fry until hot. Sprinkle over nuts; serve with lime wedges, if you like.

preparation time 10 minutes **cooking time** 15 minutes **serves** 4
nutritional count per serving 18.6g total fat (5.6g saturated fat); 1476kJ (353 cal); 9.6g carbohydrate; 34.8g protein; 4.2g fibre

Herbed-crumbed lamb racks

1 cup (70g) stale breadcrumbs
1 tablespoon finely chopped fresh flat-leaf parsley
2 tablespoons finely chopped fresh mint
2 teaspoons finely grated lemon rind
40g butter
2 shallots (50g), chopped finely
4 x 4 french-trimmed lamb cutlet racks (720g)
250g baby vine-ripened truss tomatoes
cooking-oil spray

1 Preheat oven to 220°C/200°C fan-forced.
2 Combine breadcrumbs, herbs and rind in a small bowl.
3 Melt butter in small frying pan; pour half the butter into breadcrumb mixture. Cook shallot in remaining butter, stirring, until soft; stir into breadcrumb mixture.
4 Place lamb and tomatoes in lightly oiled large baking dish; spray tomatoes with oil. Press breadcrumb mixture onto lamb. Roast, uncovered, in oven, about 15 minutes or until cooked as desired. Serve lamb with roasted tomatoes.

preparation time 10 minutes **cooking time** 20 minutes **serves** 4
nutritional count per serving 25g total fat (12.6g saturated fat); 1538kJ (368 cal); 13.7g carbohydrate; 21.4g protein; 1.9g fibre

Lemon grass fish with daikon salad

4 plate-size whole fish (1.5kg)
1 medium brown onion (150g), chopped coarsely
1 clove garlic, quartered
2cm piece fresh ginger (10g), quartered
10cm stick fresh lemon grass (20g), sliced thinly
2 tablespoons tamarind concentrate
1 tablespoon brown sugar
1 tablespoon sambal oelek
1 tablespoon kecap manis
2 teaspoons peanut oil
½ cup (125ml) water
1 small daikon (400g), cut into matchsticks
1 medium carrot (120g), cut into matchsticks
½ cup loosely packed fresh coriander leaves

1 Preheat oven to 200°C/180°C fan-forced.
2 Using sharp knife, score each fish three times on each side through thickest part of flesh; place fish in oiled large shallow baking dish.
3 Blend or process onion, garlic, ginger, lemon grass, tamarind, sugar, sambal and kecap manis until mixture forms a smooth paste.
4 Heat oil in small frying pan; cook paste, stirring, 5 minutes. Add the water; bring to the boil. Reduce heat; simmer, uncovered, 2 minutes.
5 Brush half the sauce inside each fish; pour remaining sauce over fish. Roast, uncovered, brushing occasionally, about 15 minutes or until fish is cooked.
6 Meanwhile, combine daikon, carrot and half the coriander in medium bowl. Serve fish sprinkled with remaining coriander, and daikon salad.

preparation time 10 minutes **cooking time** 20 minutes **serves** 4
nutritional count per serving 5g total fat (1.3g saturated);
949kJ (227 cal); 12.6g carbohydrate; 30.9g protein; 3.2g fibre
tip We used small snapper here, but you can use small bream or any other plate-sized whole fish in this recipe.

Pancetta and radicchio rigatoni

500g rigatoni pasta
6 slices pancetta (90g)
20g butter
1 medium leek (350g), sliced thinly
1 cup (250ml) cream
2 medium radicchio (400g), trimmed, sliced thinly
½ cup loosely packed fresh flat-leaf parsley leaves
2 teaspoons finely grated lemon rind
⅓ cup (80ml) lemon juice

1 Cook pasta in large saucepan of boiling water until tender.
2 Meanwhile, cook pancetta in heated oiled large frying pan until crisp.
Drain on absorbent paper; chop coarsely.
3 Melt butter in same frying pan; cook leek, stirring, until soft. Add cream;
bring to the boil. Reduce heat; simmer, uncovered, 2 minutes.
4 Add leek mixture to drained pasta with half the pancetta and remaining
ingredients; toss gently then sprinkle with remaining pancetta.

preparation time 10 minutes **cooking time** 15 minutes **serves** 4
nutritional count per serving 34.4g total fat (21.3g saturated fat);
3252kJ (778 cal); 96.9g carbohydrate; 22g protein; 8.2g fibre
tip Rigatoni is a tubular pasta with a ridged exterior; it is ideal for this
recipe because the filling clings both to the grooves on the pasta as well
as within the hollow. Penne pasta is an acceptable substitute, if you like.

Couscous, carrot and pistachio pilaf

2 cups (500ml) water
2 cups (400g) couscous
1 small red onion (100g), chopped finely
1 tablespoon olive oil
2 large carrots (360g), sliced thinly
1 cup (120g) stuffed green olives, halved
½ cup (70g) roasted unsalted pistachios, chopped coarsely
420g can chickpeas, rinsed, drained
1 cup loosely packed fresh coriander leaves
sumac dressing
⅓ cup (80ml) olive oil
½ cup (125ml) lemon juice
3 teaspoons sumac

1 Bring the water to the boil in medium saucepan. Remove from heat; stir in couscous and onion. Cover; stand about 5 minutes or until liquid is absorbed, fluffing with fork occasionally.
2 Meanwhile, heat oil in large frying pan; cook carrot, covered, about 3 minutes or until just tender. Uncover; cook 3 minutes.
3 Make sumac dressing.
4 Combine couscous mixture with carrot, dressing and remaining ingredients in large bowl.
sumac dressing Place ingredients in screw-top jar; shake well.

preparation time 15 minutes **cooking time** 10 minutes **serves** 4
nutritional count per serving 36.3g total fat (4.9g saturated fat); 3436kJ (822 cal); 95.9g carbohydrate; 22.4g protein; 11g fibre

Vietnamese duck salad

You need one whole chinese barbecued duck for this recipe. They are available from Asian food shops and chinese barbecued meat shops.

1kg chinese barbecued duck
1 small wombok (700g), shredded finely
1 large carrot (180g), grated coarsely
150g snow peas, sliced thinly lengthways
1 cup (80g) bean sprouts
¼ cup vietnamese mint leaves
lime dressing
½ cup (125ml) lime juice
2 tablespoons fish sauce
2 tablespoons grated palm sugar
2 fresh small red thai chillies, chopped finely

1 Make lime dressing.
2 Remove and discard skin and bones from duck; chop meat coarsely.
3 Combine dressing, duck and remaining ingredients in large bowl.
lime dressing Place ingredients in screw-top jar; shake well.

preparation time 30 minutes **serves** 4
nutritional count per serving 38g total fat (11.1g saturated fat);
2270kJ (543 cal); 13.1g carbohydrate; 35.2g protein; 5.3g fibre

Moroccan carrot dip

4 medium carrots (480g), chopped coarsely
2 cloves garlic, peeled
1 teaspoon ground cumin
1 tablespoon honey
2 tablespoons lemon juice
¼ cup (70g) greek-style yogurt
1 tablespoon coarsely chopped fresh coriander leaves

1 Cover carrots and garlic with water in small saucepan; bring to the boil. Reduce heat; simmer, covered, about 20 minutes or until carrots are soft. Drain.
2 Blend or process carrot mixture with cumin, honey and juice until smooth. Add yogurt; blend until smooth.
3 Sprinkle dip with coriander; serve with toasted turkish bread, cut into fingers, if you like.

preparation time 10 minutes **cooking time** 20 minutes **makes** 2 cups
nutritional count per tablespoon 0.2g total fat (0.1g saturated fat); 46kJ (11 cal); 1.9g carbohydrate; 0.3g protein; 0.5g fibre

Pear and roquefort salad

1 small french bread stick (150g), sliced thinly
100g roquefort cheese, softened
2 small pears (360g), sliced thinly
1 cup (110g) coarsely chopped roasted walnuts
1 butter lettuce, leaves separated
100g baby spinach leaves
buttermilk dressing
¼ cup (60ml) buttermilk
1 tablespoon lemon juice
1 tablespoon olive oil
½ teaspoon caster sugar
1 clove garlic, crushed

1 Preheat oven to 200°C/180°C fan-forced.
2 Place bread on oven tray; toast, in oven, until browned both sides.
3 Meanwhile, make buttermilk dressing.
4 Spread toast with cheese.
5 Place pears, nuts, lettuce and spinach leaves in large bowl with dressing; toss gently to combine. Serve salad with cheese toast.
buttermilk dressing Whisk ingredients in medium bowl.

preparation time 15 minutes **cooking time** 5 minutes **serves** 4
nutritional count per serving 33.7g total fat (7.4g saturated fat); 2082kJ (498 cal); 31.2g carbohydrate; 14.6g protein; 7.7g fibre

Peppered fillet steaks with creamy bourbon sauce

4 x 125g beef fillet steaks
2 teaspoons cracked black pepper
2 tablespoons olive oil
6 shallots (150g), sliced thinly
1 clove garlic, crushed
⅓ cup (80ml) bourbon
¼ cup (60ml) beef stock
2 teaspoons dijon mustard
300ml cream

1 Rub beef all over with the pepper. Heat half the oil in large frying pan; cook beef, uncovered, until cooked as desired. Remove from pan; cover to keep warm.
2 Heat remaining oil in same pan; cook shallot and garlic, stirring, until shallot softens. Add bourbon; stir until mixture simmers and starts to thicken. Add remaining ingredients; bring to the boil. Reduce heat; simmer, uncovered, about 5 minutes or until sauce thickens slightly.
3 Serve beef drizzled with sauce.

preparation time 5 minutes **cooking time** 15 minutes **serves** 4
nutritional count per serving 49.3g total fat (25.9g saturated fat); 2742kJ (656 cal); 13.2g carbohydrate; 28.7g protein; 0.7g fibre
tip The steaks go well with oven-baked chips and green beans.

Pork, kumara mash and apple salsa

2 large kumara (1kg), chopped coarsely
20g butter
2 tablespoons finely chopped fresh sage
4 x 200g pork butterfly steaks
1 tablespoon olive oil
2 cloves garlic, crushed
apple salsa
1 large green apple (200g), chopped finely
1 small red onion (100g), chopped finely
1 clove garlic, crushed
1 tablespoon finely chopped fresh sage
1 tablespoon olive oil

1 Make apple salsa.
2 Boil, steam or microwave kumara until tender; drain. Mash kumara with butter in large bowl until smooth; stir in half the sage.
3 Meanwhile, combine pork, oil, garlic and remaining sage in large bowl.
4 Cook pork in heated oiled grill pan until browned. Serve with mash and salsa.
apple salsa Combine ingredients in small bowl.

preparation time 10 minutes **cooking time** 20 minutes **serves** 4
nutritional count per serving 34.1g total fat (10.8g saturated fat);
3327kJ (796 cal); 65.8g carbohydrate; 51.5g protein; 9.1g fibre

Veal and asparagus with basil mayonnaise

4 x 170g veal cutlets
16 fresh basil leaves
4 slices prosciutto (60g)
340g asparagus, trimmed
1 tablespoon olive oil
basil mayonnaise
½ cup (150g) mayonnaise
⅓ cup lightly packed fresh basil leaves
1 tablespoon lemon juice

1 Preheat oven to 200°C/180°C fan-forced.
2 Oil two oven trays. Place cutlets on one tray; top with basil and prosciutto (securing with toothpick if necessary). Roast, uncovered, 20 minutes or until cutlets are cooked as desired.
3 Place asparagus on remaining tray, drizzle with oil; roast, uncovered, for last 10 minutes of cutlet cooking time.
4 Meanwhile, make basil mayonnaise.
5 Serve cutlets with asparagus and mayonnaise.
basil mayonnaise Blend or process ingredients until smooth.

preparation time 10 minutes **cooking time** 20 minutes **serves** 4
nutritional count per serving 20.8g total fat (3.3g saturated fat); 1522kJ (364 cal); 8.5g carbohydrate; 35.3g protein; 1.2g fibre

White bean dip

2 x 400g cans white beans, rinsed, drained
2 cloves garlic, crushed
2 tablespoons lemon juice
⅓ cup (80ml) olive oil
1 tablespoon fresh basil leaves

1 Blend or process beans, garlic, juice and oil until almost smooth.
2 Sprinkle dip with basil; serve with toasted turkish bread cut into pieces,
if you like.

preparation time 5 minutes **makes** 2 cups
nutritional count per tablespoon 3.1g total fat (0.4g saturated fat);
138kJ (33 cal); 0.6g carbohydrate; 0.5g protein; 0.9g fibre
tip We used cannellini beans here, but any variety of white beans such as
butter and haricot beans are also suitable for this dip.

Caesar salad with salt and pepper squid

1 tablespoon sichuan peppercorns
2 tablespoons sea salt
1 cup (200g) rice flour
600g cleaned squid hoods with tentacles
vegetable oil, for deep-frying
1 tablespoon sea salt, extra
2 baby cos lettuces (360g), leaves separated
caesar dressing
1 cup (300g) mayonnaise
1 clove garlic, crushed
2 tablespoons lime juice
1 tablespoon milk
1 teaspoon worcestershire sauce

1 Dry-fry peppercorns in small frying pan until fragrant; using mortar and pestle, crush peppercorns coarsely. Combine crushed pepper, salt and flour in medium bowl.
2 Cut squid hoods down centre to open out; score inside in a diagonal pattern then cut into thick strips. Toss squid pieces in flour mixture; shake off excess.
3 Make caesar dressing.
4 Heat oil in wok; deep-fry squid, in batches, until browned lightly. Drain on absorbent paper; sprinkle with extra salt.
5 Divide leaves among serving plates; top with squid, drizzle with dressing.
caesar dressing Whisk ingredients in small bowl.

preparation time 15 minutes **cooking time** 5 minutes **serves** 4
nutritional count per serving 34.7g total fat (4.5g saturated fat);
2688kJ (643 cal); 51g carbohydrate; 30g protein; 3.7g fibre

Vietnamese prawn rolls

50g rice vermicelli, soaked, drained
¼ small wombok (175g), shredded finely
½ cup loosely packed fresh mint leaves, torn
2 teaspoons brown sugar
2 tablespoons lime juice
500g cooked medium king prawns
12 x 21cm rice paper rounds
hoisin dipping sauce
½ cup (125ml) hoisin sauce
2 tablespoons rice vinegar

1 Cut vermicelli into random lengths; combine in medium bowl with wombok, mint, sugar and juice.
2 Shell and devein prawns; chop meat finely.
3 Make hoisin dipping sauce.
4 Dip one rice paper round into bowl of warm water until soft; place on board covered with tea towel. Top with a little of the prawn meat and noodle filling. Fold and roll to enclose filling. Repeat with remaining rounds, prawn meat and noodle filling.
5 Serve with hoisin dipping sauce.
hoisin dipping sauce Combine ingredients in small bowl.

preparation time 35 minutes **makes** 12
nutritional count per roll 0.9g total fat (0.1g saturated fat); 326kJ (78 cal); 10.8g carbohydrate; 5.5g protein; 1.7g fibre

Crab and soba salad with ginger miso dressing

270g soba noodles
1 lebanese cucumber (130g), seeded, sliced thinly
1 small red onion (100g), chopped finely
1 medium carrot (120g), cut into matchsticks
50g baby spinach leaves, sliced thinly
400g fresh crab meat
1 tablespoon drained pickled ginger, sliced thinly
ginger miso dressing
6cm piece fresh ginger (30g), chopped coarsely
2 tablespoons drained pickled ginger
2 cloves garlic
⅓ cup (100g) yellow miso paste
½ teaspoon wasabi paste
½ cup (125ml) rice vinegar
½ cup (125ml) vegetable oil
2 tablespoons water

1 Make ginger miso dressing.
2 Cook noodles in large saucepan of boiling water, uncovered, until just tender; drain. Rinse under cold water; drain.
3 Combine noodles in large bowl with cucumber, onion, carrot, spinach, half the crab and half the dressing.
4 Divide salad among serving plates; top with remaining crab, remaining dressing and pickled ginger.
ginger miso dressing Blend or process ingredients until smooth.

preparation time 10 minutes **cooking time** 20 minutes **serves** 4
nutritional count per serving 32.4g total fat (4g saturated fat);
2805kJ (671 cal); 55.9g carbohydrate; 35.9g protein; 5.9g fibre

Lime and chilli roasted snapper

4 x 500g plate-size whole snapper, cleaned
2cm piece fresh ginger (10g), sliced thinly
2 cloves garlic, sliced thinly
8 fresh kaffir lime leaves
1 fresh long red chilli, sliced thinly
2 tablespoons peanut oil
1 cup loosely packed fresh coriander leaves
chilli lime dressing
⅓ cup (80ml) sweet chilli sauce
¼ cup (60ml) fish sauce
¼ cup (60ml) lime juice
2 teaspoons peanut oil

1 Preheat oven to 240°C/220°C fan-forced.
2 Rinse fish inside and out under cold water; pat dry with absorbent paper.
3 Divide ginger, garlic, lime leaves and chilli among fish cavities; rub fish all over with oil.
4 Place fish in two oiled shallow baking dishes; roast, uncovered, about 15 minutes or until cooked through.
5 Meanwhile, make chilli lime dressing.
6 Drizzle fish with dressing, sprinkle with coriander leaves. Serve with steamed asian greens, if you like.
chilli lime dressing Place ingredients in screw-top jar; shake well.

preparation time 15 minutes **cooking time** 15 minutes **serves** 4
nutritional count per serving 15.1g total fat (3.5g saturated fat); 1354kJ (324 cal); 55g carbohydrate; 40.6g protein; 1.8g fibre

285

Chicken margherita

550g baby vine-ripened truss tomatoes
4 x 200g chicken breast fillets
⅓ cup (90g) basil pesto
180g bocconcini cheese, sliced thinly
20g baby spinach leaves
8 slices prosciutto (120g)

1 Preheat oven to 220°C/200°C fan-forced.
2 Remove four tomatoes from truss; slice thinly.
3 Split one chicken fillet in half horizontally; open out. Spread one tablespoon of pesto on one side of chicken fillet; top with a quarter of the cheese, a quarter of the sliced tomato and a quarter of the spinach. Fold chicken fillet over filling; wrap with two slices prosciutto to enclose securely. Repeat process with remaining chicken, pesto, cheese, sliced tomato, spinach and prosciutto.
4 Roast chicken and remaining tomatoes in oiled large shallow baking dish, uncovered, about 20 minutes or until cooked through. Serve chicken with roasted tomatoes.

preparation time 15 minutes **cooking time** 20 minutes **serves** 4
nutritional count per serving 28.7g total fat (10.5g saturated fat); 2144kJ (513 cal); 3g carbohydrate; 59.7g protein; 2.3g fibre

Lamb, bocconcini and gremolata stacks

4 x 150g lamb leg steaks
1 tablespoon olive oil
1 large red capsicum (350g)
2 tablespoons lemon juice
100g bocconcini cheese, sliced thinly
gremolata
2 teaspoons finely grated lemon rind
2 cloves garlic, chopped finely
2 tablespoons finely chopped fresh basil

1 Preheat grill.
2 Make gremolata.
3 Using meat mallet, gently pound lamb between sheets of plastic wrap until 1cm thick. Heat oil in large frying pan; cook lamb, in batches, until cooked as desired. Place lamb on oven tray.
4 Meanwhile, quarter capsicum, discard seeds and membranes. Roast under grill, skin-side up, until skin blisters and blackens. Cover capsicum pieces in plastic or paper for 5 minutes; peel away skin then slice thickly. Combine capsicum and juice in small bowl.
5 Divide capsicum and cheese among lamb steaks; grill about 5 minutes or until cheese melts. Serve stacks sprinkled with gremolata and, if you like, a salad of baby rocket leaves.
gremolata Combine ingredients in small bowl.

preparation time 15 minutes **cooking time** 20 minutes **serves** 4
nutritional count per serving 16.7g total fat (6.8g saturated fat); 1346kJ (322 cal); 3.4g carbohydrate; 38.8g protein; 1.2g fibre

Veal scaloppine with salsa verde

Veal schnitzel is available crumbed or plain (uncrumbed); we use plain uncrumbed schnitzel, sometimes called escalopes, in our recipes.

2 tablespoons olive oil
8 veal schnitzels (800g)
salsa verde
1 cup coarsely chopped fresh flat-leaf parley
½ cup finely chopped fresh dill
½ cup finely chopped fresh chives
2 tablespoons wholegrain mustard
⅓ cup (80ml) olive oil
¼ cup (60ml) lemon juice
¼ cup (50g) rinsed, drained baby capers
2 cloves garlic, crushed

1 Make salsa verde.
2 Heat oil in large frying pan; cook veal, in batches, until browned both sides and cooked as desired.
3 Serve veal topped with salsa verde. Serve with steamed baby new potatoes, if you like.
salsa verde Combine ingredients in medium bowl.

preparation time 15 minutes **cooking time** 5 minutes **serves** 4
nutritional count per serving 32.4g total fat (5.3g saturated fat); 2002kJ (479 cal); 2.2g carbohydrate; 44g protein; 1.6g fibre

Cranberry and pine nut pilaf with chicken

30g butter
1 tablespoon olive oil
1 medium brown onion (150g), chopped finely
1 stalk celery (150g), trimmed, chopped finely
1½ cups (300g) basmati rice, rinsed, drained
1 bay leaf
1 cinnamon stick
1 litre (4 cups) chicken stock
⅔ cup (160ml) water
400g chicken breast fillets
1 cup (250ml) dry white wine
⅓ cup (45g) dried cranberries
30g butter, extra
⅓ cup (50g) roasted pine nuts
1 tablespoon lemon juice

1 Melt butter with half the oil in medium saucepan; cook onion and celery, stirring, until celery softens. Add rice, bay leaf and cinnamon stick; cook, stirring, 2 minutes. Add stock and the water; bring to the boil. Reduce heat; simmer, covered, about 15 minutes or until rice is tender and liquid is absorbed.
2 Meanwhile, heat remaining oil in large frying pan. Cook chicken until browned and cooked through. Remove from heat. Cover to keep warm.
3 Pour wine into same pan; bring to the boil. Reduce heat; simmer, uncovered, until liquid is reduced by half. Stir in cranberries and extra butter; add to rice mixture, stir until combined.
4 Fluff pilaf with fork; stir in nuts and juice. Serve with sliced chicken.

preparation time 15 minutes **cooking time** 20 minutes **serves** 4
nutritional count per serving 29.5g total fat (10.5g saturated fat); 3068kJ (734 cal); 72.2g carbohydrate; 33.2g protein; 2.7g fibre

Caesar-style potato salad

2kg potatoes, chopped coarsely
25g butter
½ cup (35g) stale bread slices, cut into 1cm cubes
2 stalks celery (300g), trimmed, sliced thinly
1 cup (180g) cornichons, halved lengthways
caesar dressing
⅔ cup (190g) mayonnaise
2 tablespoons dijon mustard
1 clove garlic, crushed
2 tablespoons lemon juice
1 tablespoon worcestershire sauce
1 tablespoon milk

1 Boil, steam or microwave potato until tender; drain.
2 Meanwhile, make caesar dressing.
3 Melt butter in small frying pan; cook bread over low heat, stirring, until browned lightly.
4 Combine potato, celery, cornichons and dressing in large bowl; sprinkle with croûtons.
caesar dressing Whisk ingredients in small bowl until combined.

preparation time 15 minutes **cooking time** 10 minutes **serves** 4
nutritional count per serving 21.5g total fat (5.4g saturated fat); 2508kJ (600 cal); 80.9g carbohydrate; 14.3g protein; 12.2g fibre

Sake chicken

800g chicken breast fillets
½ cup (125ml) cooking sake
1 clove garlic, crushed
1 fresh long red chilli, chopped finely
2 tablespoons rice vinegar
2 tablespoons japanese soy sauce
1 tablespoon lemon juice
2 teaspoons sesame oil
1 teaspoon caster sugar
2 green onions, sliced thinly
2 tablespoons pickled ginger, shredded finely

1 Combine chicken, sake, garlic, chilli, vinegar, sauce, juice, oil and sugar in large frying pan; bring to the boil. Reduce heat; simmer, covered, about 10 minutes or until chicken is cooked through. Remove from heat; stand chicken in poaching liquid 10 minutes before slicing thickly. Cover to keep warm.
2 Bring poaching liquid to the boil; boil, uncovered, about 5 minutes or until sauce thickens. Serve chicken drizzled with sauce, topped with onion and ginger. Serve with steamed rice, if you like.

preparation time 10 minutes **cooking time** 15 minutes **serves** 4
nutritional count per serving 13.4g total fat (3.7g saturated); 1413kJ (338cal); 2.9g carbohydrate; 43.6g protein; 0.4g fibre

Lamb racks with mustard maple glaze

4 x 4 french-trimmed lamb cutlet racks (720g)
2 cloves garlic, sliced thinly
2 medium parsnips (500g), cut into 2cm cubes
2 small kumara (500g), cut into 2cm cubes
½ cup loosely packed fresh flat-leaf parsley leaves
mustard maple glaze
50g butter
⅓ cup (80ml) maple syrup
2 tablespoons wholegrain mustard

1 Preheat oven to 200°C/180°C fan-forced.
2 Make mustard maple glaze.
3 Using sharp knife, make cuts in lamb; press garlic slices into cuts. Place lamb in oiled large baking dish; brush with 2 tablespoons of the glaze.
4 Combine remaining glaze, parsnip and kumara in medium bowl. Place vegetables in baking dish with lamb; roast, uncovered, about 15 minutes or until vegetables are tender and lamb is cooked as desired. Stir parsley into vegetables; serve with lamb.
mustard maple glaze Cook ingredients in small saucepan, stirring, until slightly thickened.

preparation time 10 minutes **cooking time** 20 minutes **serves** 4
nutritional count per serving 26.2g total fat (13.8g saturated fat); 2153kJ (515 cal); 44.4g carbohydrate; 22.8g protein; 5.5g fibre

Warm pasta, pea and ricotta salad

375g orecchiette pasta
1½ cups (200g) frozen baby peas
½ cup coarsely chopped fresh mint
100g shaved ham, chopped coarsely
1 teaspoon finely grated lemon rind
200g ricotta cheese, crumbled
buttermilk aïoli
⅓ cup (100g) mayonnaise
2 tablespoons buttermilk
2 teaspoons lemon juice
1 clove garlic, crushed
1 teaspoon finely grated lemon rind

1 Cook pasta in large saucepan of boiling water until just tender; drain.
2 Boil, steam or microwave peas until tender; drain.
3 Meanwhile, make buttermilk aïoli.
4 Combine warm pasta, peas, mint, ham, rind and aioli in large bowl.
Serve salad sprinkled with cheese.
buttermilk aïoli Combine ingredients in small bowl.

preparation time 10 minutes **cooking time** 15 minutes **serves** 4
nutritional count per serving 16.2g total fat (5.2g saturated fat);
2328kJ (557 cal); 74.5g carbohydrate; 24.3g protein; 6.8g fibre
tip Use penne, the quill-shaped pasta, if you can't find orecchiette.

Steamed asian greens with char siu sauce

1 fresh long red chilli, sliced thinly
350g broccolini, trimmed
150g snow peas, trimmed
2 baby buk choy (300g), halved
2 tablespoons char siu sauce
2 teaspoons sesame oil
1 tablespoon peanut oil
1 tablespoon toasted sesame seeds

1 Layer chilli, broccolini, snow peas and buk choy in baking-paper-lined bamboo steamer. Steam, covered, over wok of simmering water about 5 minutes or until vegetables are just tender.
2 Combine vegetables, sauce and sesame oil in large bowl.
3 Heat peanut oil in small saucepan until hot; pour oil over vegetable mixture then toss to combine. Serve sprinkled with seeds.

preparation time 5 minutes **cooking time** 10 minutes **serves** 4
nutritional count per serving 9.5g total fat (1.4g saturated fat);
635kJ (152 cal); 7g carbohydrate; 6.6g protein; 6.6g fibre

Kaffir lime and rice salad with tofu and cashews

We used cryovac-packed ready-to-serve sweet chilli tofu in this recipe; various flavours of already marinated tofu pieces can be found in the refrigerated section of most supermarkets and Asian food stores.

2 cups (400g) jasmine rice
2 fresh kaffir lime leaves, chopped finely
2 fresh long red chillies, chopped finely
2cm piece fresh ginger (10g), grated
400g packaged marinated tofu pieces, sliced thickly
½ cup coarsely chopped fresh coriander
1 large carrot (180g), cut into matchsticks
3 green onions, sliced thinly
¾ cup (120g) roasted unsalted cashews, chopped coarsely
lime and palm sugar dressing
1 teaspoon finely grated lime rind
½ cup (125ml) lime juice
2 tablespoons grated palm sugar
2 tablespoons fish sauce

1 Cook rice in large saucepan of boiling water until tender; drain. Rinse under cold water; drain.
2 Meanwhile, make lime and palm sugar dressing.
3 Combine rice, lime leaves, chilli, ginger, tofu, coriander, carrot, half the onion, ½ cup nuts and dressing in large bowl. Serve salad sprinkled with remaining onion and nuts.
lime and palm sugar dressing Place ingredients in screw-top jar; shake well.

preparation time 20 minutes **cooking time** 10 minutes **serves** 4
nutritional count per serving 22.2g total fat (3.7g saturated fat); 2847kJ (681 cal); 90.9g carbohydrate; 25.6g protein; 6.3g fibre

Radicchio, pumpkin and haloumi salad

1kg piece pumpkin, cut into 12 wedges
180g haloumi cheese
1 medium radicchio (200g), trimmed, leaves separated
½ cup firmly packed fresh flat-leaf parsley leaves
¼ cup (50g) roasted pepitas
dressing
¼ cup (60ml) lemon juice
2 tablespoons olive oil
1 tablespoon rinsed, drained baby capers

1 Boil, steam or microwave pumpkin until tender; drain.
2 Cut cheese horizontally into four slices, cut each slice into four triangles.
3 Cook pumpkin and cheese, in batches, on heated oiled grill plate (or grill or barbecue) until browned.
4 Meanwhile, make dressing.
5 Combine radicchio in large bowl with dressing and parsley. Divide salad among serving plates; top with pumpkin, cheese and pepitas.
dressing Place ingredients in screw-top jar; shake well.

preparation time 10 minutes **cooking time** 20 minutes **serves** 4
nutritional count per serving 22g total fat (6.8g saturated fat); 1363kJ (326 cal); 15.2g carbohydrate; 14.8g protein; 5.2g fibre

Spicy carrot and zucchini bhaji

Grated zucchini can release a lot of water; if bhaji batter becomes runny, add enough besan flour to restore the batter to its original consistency.

1 cup (150g) besan (chickpea) flour
2 teaspoons coarse cooking salt
½ cup (125ml) cold water
¼ teaspoon ground turmeric
1 teaspoon chilli powder
1 teaspoon garam masala
2 cloves garlic, crushed
2 small brown onions (160g), sliced thinly
1 medium carrot (120g), grated coarsely
1 medium zucchini (120g), grated coarsely
½ cup loosely packed fresh coriander leaves
vegetable oil, for deep-frying
1 cup (320g) mango chutney

1 Whisk flour, salt and the water in medium bowl until mixture forms a smooth thick batter. Stir in spices, garlic, onion, carrot, zucchini and coriander.
2 Heat oil in wok; deep-fry tablespoons of mixture, in batches, until vegetables are tender and bhaji are browned lightly. Drain on absorbent paper. Serve with chutney.

preparation time 15 minutes **cooking time** 15 minutes **makes** 20
nutritional count per bhaji 2.3g total fat (0.3g saturated fat); 330kJ (79 cal); 12.1g carbohydrate; 2g protein; 1.6g fibre

Sichuan eggplant, almond and wombok stir-fry

⅓ cup (55g) blanched almonds, halved
1 tablespoon peanut oil
1 medium brown onion (150g), chopped coarsely
2 cloves garlic, crushed
1 fresh small red thai chilli, chopped finely
12 baby eggplants (720g), sliced thickly
150g snake beans, trimmed, chopped coarsely
1 small wombok (700g), trimmed, chopped coarsely
2 teaspoons sichuan peppercorns, crushed coarsely
¼ cup (60ml) vegetable stock
2 tablespoons hoisin sauce
1 tablespoon dark soy sauce
1 tablespoon red wine vinegar
½ cup loosely packed thai basil leaves
1 fresh long red chilli, sliced thinly

1 Stir-fry nuts in heated wok until browned lightly; remove from wok.
2 Heat oil in wok; stir-fry onion, garlic and chopped chilli until onion softens. Add eggplant and beans; stir-fry until tender. Add wombok; stir-fry until wilted.
3 Add pepper, stock, sauces and vinegar to wok; stir-fry until hot. Remove from heat; stir in basil. Serve sprinkled with nuts and sliced chilli.

preparation time 15 minutes **cooking time** 20 minutes **serves** 4
nutritional count per serving 13.6g total fat (1.4g saturated);
982kJ (235cal); 13.9g carbohydrate; 9.3g protein; 10.7g fibre

Coconut-poached fish with spinach

1½ cups (300g) jasmine rice
2 x 400ml cans coconut milk
3cm piece fresh ginger (15g), sliced thinly
1 clove garlic, sliced thinly
1 tablespoon fish sauce
1 tablespoon brown sugar
2 teaspoons sambal oelek
4 x 180g firm white fish fillets
250g frozen spinach, thawed, drained
2 tablespoons lime juice
2 green onions, sliced thinly
2 tablespoons fried shallots

1 Cook rice in large saucepan of boiling water until tender; drain.
2 Meanwhile, combine coconut milk, ginger, garlic, sauce, sugar and sambal in large frying pan; bring to the boil. Reduce heat; simmer, uncovered, 10 minutes. Add fish; simmer, covered, about 10 minutes or until fish is cooked. Remove fish from pan.
3 Add spinach and juice to pan; cook, stirring, until hot.
4 Serve fish with coconut spinach and rice; sprinkle over green onion and fried shallots.

preparation time 10 minutes **cooking time** 25 minutes **serves** 4
nutritional count per serving 46.6g total fat (37.7g saturated fat); 3795kJ (908 cal); 71.9g carbohydrate; 47.5g protein; 6.2g fibre
tip Use any boneless firm white fish fillets you like — blue eye, bream swordfish, ling, whiting or sea perch are all good choices.

Passionfruit soufflés

10g butter, softened
1 tablespoon caster sugar
2 eggs, separated
170g can passionfruit in syrup
⅔ cup (110g) icing sugar
4 egg whites
1 tablespoon icing sugar, extra, for dusting

1 Preheat oven to 220°C/200°C fan-forced. Grease four 1-cup (250ml) soufflé dishes with butter; sprinkle with caster sugar, shake away excess.
2 Combine egg yolks, passionfruit and half the sifted icing sugar in large bowl.
3 Beat egg whites in small bowl with electric mixer until soft peaks form; add remaining sifted icing sugar, beat until firm peaks form. Gently fold a third of the egg-white mixture into passionfruit mixture, then fold in remaining egg-white mixture.
4 Place dishes on oven tray. Spoon soufflé mixture into dishes; bake about 12 minutes or until soufflés are puffed and golden. Dust with extra sifted icing sugar; serve immediately.

preparation time 10 minutes **cooking time** 12 minutes **makes** 4
nutritional count per soufflé 4.8g total fat (2.2g saturated fat); 995kJ (238 cal); 37.3g carbohydrate; 8.2g protein; 5.9g fibre

Balsamic strawberries with mascarpone

500g strawberries, halved
¼ cup (55g) caster sugar
2 tablespoons balsamic vinegar
1 cup (250g) mascarpone cheese
1 tablespoon icing sugar
1 teaspoon vanilla extract
¼ cup coarsely chopped fresh mint

1 Combine strawberries, caster sugar and vinegar in medium bowl, cover; refrigerate 20 minutes.
2 Meanwhile, combine mascarpone, icing sugar and extract in small bowl.
3 Stir mint into strawberry mixture; divide among serving dishes. Serve with mascarpone mixture.

preparation time 5 minutes (plus refrigeration time) **serves** 4
nutritional count per serving 29.8g total fat (20.3g saturated fat); 1572kJ (376 cal); 21.2g carbohydrate; 5.2g protein; 3g fibre

Pear, chocolate and almond galette

80g dark cooking chocolate, chopped finely
¼ cup (30g) almond meal
1 sheet ready-rolled puff pastry
1 tablespoon milk
1 medium pear (230g)
1 tablespoon raw sugar

1 Preheat oven to 220°C/200°C fan-forced. Line oven tray with baking paper.
2 Combine chocolate and 2 tablespoons of the almond meal in small bowl.
3 Cut pastry sheet into quarters; place on tray, prick each quarter with a fork, then brush with milk. Divide chocolate mixture among pastry squares, leaving a 2cm border.
4 Peel and core pear; cut into quarters. Cut each quarter into thin slices. Spread one sliced pear quarter across each pastry square; sprinkle with sugar then remaining almond meal.
5 Bake about 15 minutes or until pastry is golden brown.

preparation time 5 minutes **cooking time** 15 minutes **serves** 4
nutritional count per serving 19.9g total fat (11g saturated fat); 1480kJ (354 cal); 38.4g carbohydrate; 5g protein; 3.5g fibre

Pavlova trifle

You need 6 passionfruit to get the required amount of pulp for this recipe. Packaged mini pavlova shells are sold in supermarkets.

¾ cup (180ml) thickened cream
2 tablespoons icing sugar
200g crème fraîche
250g strawberries, quartered
2 medium bananas (400g), sliced thickly
½ cup (125ml) passionfruit pulp
50g mini pavlova shells, chopped coarsely
3 medium kiwifruits (255g), chopped coarsely

1 Beat cream and icing sugar in small bowl with electric mixer until soft peaks form; stir in crème fraîche.
2 Divide strawberries and banana among four 1½-cup (375ml) glasses. Top with half the passionfruit pulp.
3 Divide crème fraîche mixture among glasses; top with meringue, kiwifruit and remaining passionfruit pulp.

preparation time 25 minutes **serves** 4
nutritional count per serving 36.9g total fat (24.1g saturated fat); 1994kJ (477 cal); 27.1g carbohydrate; 5.7g protein; 8.5g fibre

Citrus salad with lime and mint granita

2 medium oranges (480g)
2 small pink grapefruit (700g)
⅓ cup finely chopped fresh mint
2 tablespoons icing sugar
1 tablespoon lime juice
2 cups ice cubes

1 Segment orange and grapefruit into medium bowl.
2 Blend or process mint, sugar, juice and ice until ice is crushed;
serve with fruit.

preparation time 15 minutes **serves** 4
nutritional count per serving 0.4g total fat (0g saturated fat);
385kJ (92 cal); 18.1g carbohydrate; 2.1g protein; 2.7g fibre

Brandy snap and rhubarb stacks

You need about 5 trimmed stems of rhubarb for this recipe.

3¼ cups (400g) coarsely chopped rhubarb
2 tablespoons water
¼ cup (55g) caster sugar
30g butter
2 tablespoons brown sugar
1 tablespoon golden syrup
½ teaspoon ground ginger
2 tablespoons plain flour
¼ cup (70g) yogurt

1 Preheat oven to 180°C/160°C fan-forced. Grease two oven trays.

2 Combine rhubarb, the water and caster sugar in medium saucepan; bring to the boil. Reduce heat; simmer, uncovered, stirring occasionally, about 5 minutes or until rhubarb softens. Drain rhubarb mixture through sieve over medium bowl; reserve liquid. Spread rhubarb mixture onto metal tray; cover with foil, place in the freezer.

3 Meanwhile, combine butter, brown sugar, syrup and ginger in same cleaned pan; stir over low heat until butter has melted. Remove from heat, stir in flour.

4 Drop level teaspoons of the mixture about 6cm apart onto trays. Bake, in oven, about 7 minutes or until brandy snaps bubble and become golden brown; cool on trays for 2 minutes then transfer to wire rack to cool completely.

5 Place cooled rhubarb mixture in small bowl; add yogurt, pull skewer backwards and forwards through rhubarb mixture for marbled effect.

6 Sandwich three brandy snaps with a quarter of the rhubarb mixture; repeat with remaining brandy snaps and rhubarb mixture.

7 Place stacks on serving plates; drizzle with reserved rhubarb liquid.

preparation time 10 minutes **cooking time** 15 minutes **serves** 4
nutritional count per serving 7g total fat (4.5g saturated fat);
865kJ (207 cal); 31.7g carbohydrate; 3g protein; 3.4g fibre
tip Placing the softened rhubarb in the freezer is to quickly cool the mixture, not freeze it. Cooked frozen rhubarb is also available at most supermarkets.

Hazelnut tiramisu

1 tablespoon instant coffee granules
2 tablespoons caster sugar
⅔ cup (160ml) boiling water
⅓ cup (80ml) hazelnut-flavoured liqueur
½ cup (125ml) cream
1 cup (250g) mascarpone cheese
12 sponge-finger biscuits (140g)
¼ cup (25g) coarsely grated dark chocolate
½ cup (70g) coarsely chopped roasted hazelnuts

1 Dissolve coffee and half the sugar in the water in medium heatproof bowl. Stir in liqueur; cool 10 minutes.
2 Meanwhile, beat cream and remaining sugar in small bowl with electric mixer until soft peaks form; fold in mascarpone.
3 Dip biscuits, one at a time, into coffee mixture; place, in a single layer, in shallow 2-litre (8-cup) serving dish. Pour any remaining coffee mixture over biscuits. Spread cream mixture over biscuits; sprinkle with combined chocolate and nuts. Refrigerate until required.

preparation time 20 minutes **serves** 6
nutritional count per serving 40.5g total fat (22.2g saturated fat); 2153kJ (515 cal); 24.5g carbohydrate; 7g protein; 2g fibre

Berry, coconut and yogurt parfaits

1 cup (150g) frozen mixed berries
1 tablespoon caster sugar
1 tablespoon coconut-flavoured liqueur
1 cup (250ml) raspberry and cranberry juice
12 sponge-finger biscuits (140g)
500g vanilla yogurt
2 tablespoons flaked coconut, toasted

1 Blend or process frozen berries, sugar, liqueur and ¼ cup of juice until smooth.
2 Dip biscuits in remaining juice; divide among six 1½-cup (375ml) serving glasses.
3 Divide half the yogurt among glasses; top with half the berry mixture. Repeat layering with remaining yogurt and berry mixture. Sprinkle with toasted coconut.

preparation time 10 minutes **serves** 6
nutritional count per serving 5.2g total fat (3.3g saturated fat); 882kJ (211 cal); 31.5g carbohydrate; 6.5g protein; 1.1g fibre
tip Do not defrost the berries before blending.

Passionfruit and banana sundae

You need 6 passionfruit to get the required amount of pulp for this recipe. Packaged mini pavlova shells are sold in supermarkets.

300ml thickened cream
2 tablespoons lemon-flavoured spread
50g mini pavlova shells, chopped coarsely
½ cup (125ml) passionfruit pulp
4 small bananas (520g), chopped coarsely

1 Beat cream and spread in small bowl with electric mixer until soft peaks form.
2 Layer lemon cream, pavlova pieces, passionfruit and banana among four serving glasses.

preparation time 5 minutes **cooking time** 10 minutes **serves** 4
nutritional count per serving 28.6g total fat (18.5g saturated fat); 1839kJ (440 cal); 38.9g carbohydrate; 4.4g protein; 6.3g fibre

Mango galettes with coconut cream

1 sheet ready-rolled puff pastry, quartered
20g butter, melted
2 firm medium mangoes (860g), halved, sliced thinly
1 tablespoon brown sugar
⅔ cup (160ml) thickened cream, whipped
2 teaspoons coconut-flavoured liqueur
⅓ cup (15g) flaked coconut, toasted

1 Preheat oven to 200°C/180°C fan-forced. Grease oven tray; line with baking paper.
2 Place pastry squares on oven tray, prick with fork; brush with half the melted butter. Divide mango among pastry squares, leaving a 2cm border. Sprinkle sugar over galettes; drizzle with remaining butter.
3 Bake galettes, uncovered, about 15 minutes.
4 Meanwhile, combine remaining ingredients in small bowl.
5 Serve galettes with coconut cream.

preparation time 10 minutes **cooking time** 15 minutes **serves** 4
nutritional count per serving 31.2g total fat (19.7g saturated fat); 1969kJ (471 cal); 40.1g carbohydrate; 5g protein; 3.4g fibre

Walnut and ricotta-stuffed figs

8 medium figs (480g)
¼ cup (25g) roasted walnuts, chopped coarsely
½ cup (120g) ricotta cheese
1 tablespoon caster sugar
caramel sauce
⅓ cup (80ml) cream
30g butter
⅓ cup (75g) firmly packed brown sugar

1 Preheat oven to 200°C/180°C fan-forced.
2 Cut figs, from the top, into quarters, being careful not to cut all the way through; open slightly. Place on oven tray.
3 Combine nuts, cheese and sugar in small bowl; divide nut mixture among figs. Cook, uncovered, about 10 minutes or until figs are heated through.
4 Meanwhile, make caramel sauce.
5 Place two figs in each serving dish; drizzle with caramel sauce.
caramel sauce Stir ingredients in small saucepan over heat until sugar dissolves. Simmer, uncovered, 3 minutes.

preparation time 10 minutes **cooking time** 10 minutes **serves** 4
nutritional count per serving 22.8g total fat (12.2g saturated fat); 1526kJ (365 cal); 32.6g carbohydrate; 6g protein; 3.1g fibre

fast
barbecues

Greek salad with grilled lamb

¼ cup (70g) yogurt
⅓ cup (80ml) lemon juice
¼ cup (60ml) olive oil
2 cloves garlic, crushed
600g lamb fillets
3 medium tomatoes (450g), cut into thin wedges
1 small red onion (100g), sliced thinly
2 medium red capsicums (400g), chopped coarsely
2 lebanese cucumbers (260g), chopped coarsely
½ cup (75g) seeded kalamata olives
400g can chickpeas, rinsed, drained
1 cup firmly packed fresh flat-leaf parsley leaves
100g fetta cheese, crumbled

1 Combine yogurt, 1 tablespoon of the juice, 1 tablespoon of the oil and half the garlic in medium bowl, add lamb; mix well.
2 Meanwhile, combine remaining juice, oil and garlic in screw-top jar; shake well.
3 Drain lamb; cook on heated oiled grill plate (or grill or barbecue) until cooked as desired. Cover; stand 5 minutes then slice thickly.
4 Combine remaining ingredients in large bowl with lemon dressing. Serve salad topped with lamb.

preparation time 20 minutes **cooking time** 5 minutes **serves** 4
nutritional count per serving 27.5g total fat (8.8g saturated fat); 2215kJ (530 cal); 23.1g carbohydrate; 44g protein; 7.8g fibre

Tandoori lamb cutlets with fresh melon and coconut chutney

¼ cup (75g) tandoori paste
¼ cup (70g) yogurt
12 french-trimmed lamb cutlets (600g)
1 cup (110g) coarsely grated fresh coconut
½ large firm honeydew melon (850g), grated coarsely, drained
2 tablespoons finely chopped fresh mint
1 tablespoon lemon juice

1 Combine paste, yogurt and lamb in large bowl; turn to coat in tandoori mixture. Cook lamb on heated oiled grill plate (or grill or barbecue) until browned both sides and cooked as desired.
2 Meanwhile, combine coconut, melon, mint and juice in medium bowl. Serve coconut chutney with lamb and, if desired, pappadums and lemon wedges.

preparation time 15 minutes **cooking time** 10 minutes **serves** 4
nutritional count per serving 27.3g total fat (13.5g saturated fat); 1601kJ (383 cal); 13.2g carbohydrate; 18.9g protein; 5.7g fibre
tips If fresh coconut is unavailable, use 1 cup finely shredded dried coconut. To open a fresh coconut, pierce one of the eyes then roast coconut briefly in a very hot oven only until cracks appear in the shell. Cool then break the coconut apart and grate or flake the firm white flesh. The chutney is best if made with a firm (just underripe) honeydew melon.

Minty lamb cutlets with mixed vegie smash

1 tablespoon finely chopped fresh mint
⅓ cup (110g) mint jelly
1 teaspoon finely grated lemon rind
2 teaspoons olive oil
8 french-trimmed lamb cutlets (400g)
mixed vegie smash
600g baby new potatoes, halved
2 large carrots (360g), cut into 2cm pieces
1 cup (120g) frozen peas
1 tablespoon olive oil
1 tablespoon lemon juice
2 tablespoons finely chopped fresh mint

1 Make mixed vegie smash.
2 Combine mint and jelly in small bowl.
3 Rub combined rind and oil over lamb; cook lamb on heated oiled grill plate (or grill or barbecue) until cooked as desired.
4 Serve lamb with smash and mint mixture.
mixed vegie smash Boil, steam or microwave potato, carrot and peas, separately, until tender; drain. Crush potato and peas roughly in large bowl; stir in carrot and remaining ingredients.

preparation time 10 minutes **cooking time** 25 minutes **serves** 4
nutritional count per serving 15.8g total fat (4.9g saturated fat);
1572kJ (376 cal); 38.4g carbohydrate; 16.3g protein; 7.3g fibre

Thai fish burgers

We used blue-eye in this recipe, but any firm white fish fillets can be used.

500g firm white fish fillets, chopped coarsely
1 tablespoon fish sauce
1 tablespoon kecap manis
1 clove garlic, quartered
1 fresh small red thai chilli, chopped coarsely
50g green beans, trimmed, chopped coarsely
¼ cup (20g) fried shallots
¼ cup coarsely chopped fresh coriander
60g baby spinach leaves
1 lebanese cucumber (130g), seeded, sliced thinly
1 tablespoon lime juice
2 teaspoons brown sugar
2 teaspoons fish sauce, extra
4 hamburger buns (360g)
⅓ cup (80ml) sweet chilli sauce

1 Blend or process fish, sauce, kecap manis, garlic and chilli until smooth. Combine fish mixture in large bowl with beans, shallots and coriander; shape into four patties.
2 Cook patties on heated oiled flat plate about 15 minutes or until cooked.
3 Combine spinach, cucumber, juice, sugar and extra sauce in medium bowl.
4 Split buns in half; toast cut sides. Sandwich salad, patties and sweet chilli sauce between bun halves.

preparation time 20 minutes **cooking time** 15 minutes **serves** 4
nutritional count per serving 5.3g total fat (0.7g saturated fat); 1722kJ (412 cal); 55.2g carbohydrate; 32g protein; 5.7g fibre

Seafood in lemon cream sauce

500g uncooked medium king prawns
250g scallops, roe removed
2 teaspoons olive oil
3 cloves garlic, crushed
340g asparagus, halved crossways
150g sugar snap peas, trimmed
2 teaspoons lemon juice
2 tablespoons dry white wine
¾ cup (180ml) cream
2 tablespoons coarsely chopped fresh parsley

1 Shell and devein prawns, leaving tails intact; combine with scallops, oil and garlic in medium bowl.
2 Cook seafood on heated oiled grill plate (or grill or barbecue) until changed in colour. Remove from heat; cover to keep warm.
3 Meanwhile, boil, steam or microwave asparagus and peas, separately, until tender. Drain; cover to keep warm.
4 Simmer juice and wine in small saucepan, uncovered, about 1 minute or until liquid is reduced by half. Add cream; bring to the boil. Reduce heat; simmer, uncovered, 2 minutes. Add seafood; simmer, uncovered, until hot.
5 Serve seafood with vegetables; sprinkle with chopped parsley.

preparation time 15 minutes **cooking time** 10 minutes **serves** 4
nutritional count per serving 22.7g total fat (13.4g saturated fat);
1367kJ (327 cal); 4.6g carbohydrate; 23.7g protein; 2.2g fibre

Piri piri chicken thigh fillets

4 fresh long red chillies, chopped coarsely
1 teaspoon dried chilli flakes
2 cloves garlic, quartered
1 teaspoon sea salt
2 tablespoons olive oil
1 tablespoon cider vinegar
2 teaspoons brown sugar
8 x 125g thigh fillets

1 Using mortar and pestle, grind fresh chilli, chilli flakes, garlic and salt to make piri piri paste.
2 Combine paste with oil, vinegar, sugar and chicken in medium bowl. Cook chicken on heated oiled grill plate (or grill or barbecue) until cooked through. Serve with lime wedges, if desired.

preparation time 10 minutes **cooking time** 15 minutes **serves** 4
nutritional count per serving 27.2g total fat (6.8g saturated fat); 1822kJ (436 cal); 1.8g carbohydrate; 46.6g protein; 0.3g fibre

Chicken yakitori with sesame dipping sauce

12 chicken tenderloins (1kg)
sesame dipping sauce
¼ cup (60ml) light soy sauce
2 tablespoons mirin
3 teaspoons white sugar
½ teaspoon sesame oil
1 teaspoon sesame seeds

1 Combine ingredients for sesame dipping sauce in small saucepan; stir over medium heat until sugar dissolves, divide dipping sauce into two portions.
2 Thread each tenderloin onto a skewer; brush skewers with one portion of the dipping sauce. Cook skewers, in batches, on heated oiled grill plate (or grill or barbecue) until chicken is cooked. Serve skewers with remaining portion of sesame dipping sauce.

preparation time 20 minutes **cooking time** 10 minutes **serves** 4
nutritional count per serving 20.4g total fat (6.4g saturated fat); 1643kJ (393 cal); 3.8g carbohydrate; 47.1g protein; 0.1g fibre
tip You need 12 bamboo skewers for this recipe; soak them in cold water for 30 minutes to prevent scorching during cooking.

Veal cutlets with green olive salsa

2 tablespoons olive oil
2 cloves garlic, crushed
1 tablespoon finely chopped fresh oregano
2 teaspoons finely grated lemon rind
1 tablespoon lemon juice
4 x 125g veal cutlets
green olive salsa
1 tablespoon lemon juice
¼ cup coarsely chopped fresh flat-leaf parsley
½ cup (80g) finely chopped large green olives
1 small green capsicum (150g), chopped finely
1 tablespoon olive oil
1 clove garlic, crushed
1 tablespoon finely chopped fresh oregano
barbecued kipflers
1.5kg kipfler potatoes
¼ cup fresh thyme leaves
1 tablespoon coarsely grated lemon rind
2 cloves crushed garlic
⅓ cup (80ml) olive oil
¼ cup (60ml) lemon juice

1 Make barbecued kipflers; make green olive salsa.
2 Meanwhile, combine oil, garlic, oregano, rind and juice in small bowl; brush mixture over veal. Cook veal on heated oiled grill plate (or grill or barbecue) until browned both sides and cooked as desired.
3 Serve veal with salsa and potatoes.
green olive salsa Combine ingredients in small bowl.
barbecued kipflers Boil, steam or microwave potatoes until tender; drain. Halve potatoes lengthways. Combine thyme, rind, garlic, oil, juice and potato in large bowl; toss to coat in mixture. Cook potato on heated oiled grill plate (or grill or barbecue) about 15 minutes or until browned.

preparation time 20 minutes **cooking time** 15 minutes **serves** 4
nutritional count per serving 35g total fat (5.3g saturated fat); 2897kJ (692 cal); 55.9g carbohydrate; 32.6g protein; 9.1g fibre

Char-grilled steak and vegetables with baba ghanoush

3 cloves garlic, crushed
2 tablespoons olive oil
2 teaspoons finely grated lemon rind
4 x 150g beef eye-fillet steaks
2 medium red capsicums (400g), sliced thickly
2 large zucchini (300g), halved crossways, sliced thinly lengthways
½ cup (120g) baba ghanoush
⅓ cup loosely packed fresh mint leaves

1 Combine garlic, oil, rind, beef, capsicum and zucchini in large bowl.
Cook beef and vegetables on heated grill plate (or grill or barbecue),
in batches, until beef is cooked as desired and vegetables are tender.
2 Divide vegetables among serving plates, top with beef. Serve with
baba ghanoush and mint.

preparation time 15 minutes **cooking time** 20 minutes **serves** 4
nutritional count per serving 17.3g total fat (4.6g saturated fat);
1354kJ (324 cal); 5.9g carbohydrate; 34.2g protein; 3.6g fibre

Grilled salmon with nam jim and herb salad

4 x 220g salmon fillets, skin-on
nam jim
3 long green chillies, chopped coarsely
2 fresh small red thai chillies, chopped coarsely
2 cloves garlic, quartered
1 shallot (25g), quartered
2cm piece fresh ginger (10g), quartered
⅓ cup (80ml) lime juice
2 tablespoons fish sauce
1 tablespoon grated palm sugar
1 tablespoon peanut oil
¼ cup (35g) roasted unsalted cashews, chopped finely
herb salad
1½ cups loosely packed fresh mint leaves
1 cup loosely packed fresh coriander leaves
1 cup loosely packed fresh basil leaves, torn
1 medium red onion (170g), sliced thinly
2 lebanese cucumbers (260g), seeded, sliced thinly

1 Make nam jim.
2 Cook salmon, on heated oiled grill plate (or grill or barbecue) until cooked as desired.
3 Meanwhile, make herb salad.
4 Serve salmon and herb salad topped with nam jim.
nam jim Blend or process chillies, garlic, shallot, ginger, juice, sauce, sugar and oil until smooth; stir in nuts.
herb salad Combine ingredients in medium bowl.

preparation time 25 minutes **cooking time** 10 minutes **serves** 4
nutritional count per serving 25g total fat (5.1g saturated fat); 1948kJ (466 cal); 10.8g carbohydrate; 47.6g protein; 4.4g fibre

357

Mexican pork cutlets with avocado salsa

2 tablespoons taco seasoning mix
¼ cup (60ml) olive oil
4 x 235g pork cutlets
3 small tomatoes (270g), seeded, chopped finely
1 small avocado (200g), chopped finely
1 lebanese cucumber (130g), seeded, chopped finely
1 tablespoon lime juice

1 Combine seasoning, 2 tablespoons of the oil and pork in large bowl.
Cook pork on heated oiled grill plate (or grill or barbecue) until cooked.
2 Meanwhile, combine remaining oil in medium bowl with tomato,
avocado, cucumber and juice. Serve pork with salsa.

preparation time 10 minutes **cooking time** 10 minutes **serves** 4
nutritional count per serving 42.2g total fat (10.7g saturated fat);
2241kJ (536 cal); 1.2g carbohydrate; 38g protein; 1.2g fibre
tip Taco seasoning mix is available from most supermarkets. It is meant
to duplicate the taste of a Mexican sauce made from cumin, oregano,
chillies and other spices.

Char-grilled radicchio parcels

3 cloves garlic, crushed
1 cup (150g) drained semi-dried tomatoes, chopped coarsely
420g bocconcini cheese
1 cup coarsely chopped fresh basil
2 x 420g cans white beans, rinsed, drained
24 large radicchio leaves
1 tablespoon balsamic vinegar

1 Combine garlic, tomato, cheese, basil and beans in large bowl.
2 Plunge radicchio into large saucepan of boiling water then drain immediately; submerge in iced water to halt cooking process. When cool, drain; pat dry with absorbent paper.
3 Slightly overlap 2 leaves; centre about a quarter cup of bean mixture on leaves then roll, folding in edges to enclose filling. Repeat with remaining bean mixture and leaves.
4 Cook parcels, seam-side down, on heated oiled grill plate (or grill or barbecue) until filling is hot. Serve parcels drizzled with vinegar.

preparation time 20 minutes **cooking time** 5 minutes **serves** 4
nutritional count per serving 20g total fat (11g saturated fat);
1659kJ (397 cal); 18.9g carbohydrate; 28.7g protein; 13.8g fibre

Herbed beef rib-eye with tapenade mash

4 large potatoes (1.2kg), chopped coarsely
1 tablespoon dried italian herbs
1 clove garlic, crushed
2 tablespoons olive oil
4 x 200g beef rib-eye steaks
½ cup (125ml) cream
2 tablespoons black olive tapenade
60g baby rocket leaves

1 Boil, steam or microwave potato until tender; drain. Cover to keep warm.
2 Meanwhile, combine herbs, garlic, oil and beef in medium bowl.
3 Cook beef on heated oiled grill plate (or grill or barbecue), brushing occasionally with herb mixture, until cooked as desired. Remove from heat, cover beef; stand 5 minutes.
4 Mash potato in large bowl with cream and tapenade. Stir in half the rocket.
5 Serve beef with mash and remaining rocket.

preparation time 10 minutes **cooking time** 25 minutes **serves** 4
nutritional count per serving 34g total fat (14.3g saturated fat); 2930kJ (761 cal); 41.1g carbohydrate; 54.6g protein; 6.4g fibre

Spiced lamb burger with tzatziki

500g lamb mince
½ small red onion (50g), chopped finely
1 egg yolk
½ cup (35g) stale breadcrumbs
2 tablespoons sumac
1 large loaf turkish bread (430g)
250g tzatziki
350g watercress, trimmed
¼ cup (60ml) lemon juice
225g can sliced beetroot, drained

1 Combine mince, onion, egg yolk, breadcrumbs and half the sumac in medium bowl; shape mixture into four patties.
2 Cook patties on heated oiled grill plate (or grill or barbecue) until cooked.
3 Meanwhile, preheat grill.
4 Trim bread then cut into quarters; halve quarters horizontally. Toast, cut-sides up, under grill.
5 Combine remaining sumac and tzatziki in small bowl. Combine watercress and juice in another bowl.
6 Sandwich patties, tzatziki mixture, beetroot and watercress between bread pieces.

preparation time 20 minutes **cooking time** 10 minutes **serves** 4
nutritional count per serving 21.1g total fat (7.5g saturated fat); 2604kJ (623 cal); 60g carbohydrate; 43.8g protein; 8g fibre
tip Tzatziki is a Greek yogurt dip made with cucumber, garlic and sometimes chopped fresh mint. You can buy tzatziki ready-made in supermarkets and delicatessens.

Pork fillet and pancetta kebabs

8 x 15cm stalks fresh rosemary
600g pork fillet, cut into 2cm pieces
8 slices pancetta (120g), halved
1 large red capsicum (350g), cut into 24 pieces
⅓ cup (80ml) olive oil
1 clove garlic, crushed

1 Remove leaves from bottom two-thirds of each rosemary stalk; reserve
2 tablespoons leaves, chop finely. Sharpen trimmed ends of stalks to a point.
2 Wrap each piece of pork in one slice of the pancetta; thread, alternately
with capsicum, onto stalks.
3 Brush kebabs with combined chopped rosemary, oil and garlic. Cook
on heated oiled grill plate (or grill or barbecue), brushing frequently with
the rosemary mixture, until cooked.
4 Serve kebabs with a greek salad, if you like.

preparation time 15 minutes **cooking time** 15 minutes **serves** 4
nutritional count per serving 23.6g total fat (4.4g saturated fat);
1601kJ (383 cal); 3.1g carbohydrate; 39.5g protein; 1g fibre

Za'atar-spiced veal loin chops with fattoush

4 x 200g veal loin chops
za'atar
1 tablespoon sumac
1 tablespoon toasted sesame seeds
2 teaspoons finely chopped fresh thyme
1 tablespoon olive oil
1 teaspoon dried marjoram
fattoush
2 large pitta breads (160g)
4 medium tomatoes (600g), cut into wedges
2 lebanese cucumbers (260g), seeded, sliced thinly
1 medium green capsicum (200g), cut into 2cm pieces
3 green onions, sliced thinly
1 cup coarsely chopped fresh flat-leaf parsley
½ cup coarsely chopped fresh mint
½ cup (125ml) olive oil
¼ cup (60ml) lemon juice
2 cloves garlic, crushed

1 Preheat grill.
2 Make za'atar.
3 Make fattoush.
4 Cook veal on heated oiled grill plate (or grill or barbecue) until browned both sides and cooked. Sprinkle about a tablespoon of the za'atar equally over the veal; serve with fattoush.
za'atar Combine ingredients in small bowl.
fattoush Grill bread until crisp; break into small pieces. Combine tomato, cucumber, capsicum, onion and herbs in large bowl. Just before serving, toss bread and combined oil, juice and garlic into salad.

preparation time 15 minutes **cooking time** 20 minutes **serves** 4
nutritional count per serving 38.9g total fat (5.9g saturated fat); 2587kJ (619 cal); 27.8g carbohydrate; 36.5g protein; 17.1g fibre
tip Za'atar can also be purchased from Middle-Eastern food shops and some delicatessens. Store what you don't use in this recipe, in a glass jar with a tight-fitting lid, in the fridge for future use.

Pesto chicken with grilled zucchini

6 medium zucchini (720g), sliced thickly lengthways
2 tablespoons olive oil
1 clove garlic, crushed
1 tablespoon finely chopped fresh basil
1 teaspoon finely grated lemon rind
⅓ cup (90g) sun-dried tomato pesto
2 tablespoons chicken stock
4 x 200g chicken thigh fillets, cut into thirds

1 Cook zucchini on heated oiled grill plate (or grill or barbecue), in batches, until tender. Combine with oil, garlic, basil and rind in medium bowl; cover to keep warm.
2 Combine pesto, stock and chicken in large bowl. Cook chicken on heated oiled grill plate (or grill or barbecue), brushing occasionally with pesto mixture, until cooked. Serve chicken with zucchini, accompany with rocket leaves, if you like.

preparation time 10 minutes **cooking time** 15 minutes **serves** 4
nutritional count per serving 33.1g total fat (7.6g saturated fat); 2611kJ (481 cal); 3.3g carbohydrate; 41.7g protein; 3.6g fibre

Teriyaki salmon with soba salad

250g dried soba noodles
4 x 200g salmon fillets
¼ cup (60ml) teriyaki sauce
2 tablespoons sweet chilli sauce
1 medium red capsicum (200g), sliced thinly
4 green onions, sliced thinly
1 tablespoon light soy sauce
2 teaspoons lime juice
1 teaspoon sesame oil

1 Cook noodles in large saucepan of boiling water until just tender; drain. Rinse under cold water; drain.

2 Meanwhile, combine salmon, teriyaki sauce, and 1 tablespoon of the sweet chilli sauce in medium bowl.

3 Cook salmon on heated oiled grill plate (or grill or barbecue), brushing occasionally with teriyaki mixture, until cooked as desired.

4 Combine noodles in large bowl with capsicum, onion, soy sauce, juice, oil and remaining sweet chilli sauce. Serve soba with salmon, and lime wedges, if you like.

preparation time 10 minutes **cooking time** 15 minutes **serves** 4
nutritional count per serving 16.4g total fat (3.5g saturated fat); 2249kJ (538 cal); 47.4g carbohydrate; 48g protein; 3.2g fibre

Grilled loin chops with apple and onion plum sauce

2 medium apples (300g)
1 tablespoon olive oil
1 medium red onion (170g), cut into thin wedges
4 x 280g pork loin chops
½ cup (125ml) plum sauce
¼ cup (60ml) lemon juice
⅓ cup (80ml) chicken stock

1 Cut each unpeeled, uncored apple horizontally into four slices. Heat oil in grill pan; cook apple and onion, turning, until softened.
2 Meanwhile, cook pork on heated oiled grill plate (or grill or barbecue) until cooked.
3 Stir sauce, juice and stock into apple mixture; simmer 1 minute. Serve pork with sauce.

preparation time 10 minutes **cooking time** 20 minutes **serves** 4
nutritional count per serving 29.7g total fat (9.1g saturated fat); 2404kJ (575 cal); 32g carbohydrate; 45g protein; 1.8g fibre

Balsamic rosemary grilled veal steaks

2 tablespoons olive oil
2 tablespoons balsamic vinegar
1 tablespoon fresh rosemary leaves
2 cloves garlic, crushed
4 x 125g veal steaks
4 medium egg tomatoes (300g), halved
4 flat mushrooms (320g)

1 Combine oil, vinegar, rosemary, garlic and veal in medium bowl.
2 Cook veal on heated oiled grill plate (or grill or barbecue), brushing occasionally with vinegar mixture, until cooked as desired. Remove from heat; cover to keep warm.
3 Cook tomato and mushrooms on heated oiled grill plate until tender. Serve veal with grilled vegetables.

preparation time 10 minutes **cooking time** 15 minutes **serves** 4
nutritional count per serving 11.3g total fat (1.8g saturated fat); 1016kJ (243 cal); 2.1g carbohydrate; 31.6g protein; 3.3g fibre

Orange and soy salmon parcels

4 x 200g salmon fillets
4 green onions, sliced thinly
1cm piece fresh ginger (5g), sliced thinly
2 cloves garlic, sliced thinly
¼ cup (60ml) light soy sauce
1 tablespoon finely grated orange rind
⅓ cup (80ml) orange juice
2 teaspoons grated palm sugar
450g baby buk choy, chopped coarsely
350g broccolini, halved crossways

1 Place each fillet on a piece of lightly oiled foil large enough to
completely enclose fish. Combine onion, ginger, garlic, sauce, rind, juice
and sugar in small jug; divide mixture among fish pieces. Gather corners
of foil above fish; twist to enclose securely.
2 Cook parcels on heated oiled grill plate (or grill or barbecue) about
5 minutes or until fish is cooked as desired.
3 Meanwhile, boil, steam or microwave buk choy and broccolini,
separately, until tender; drain. Serve salmon with vegetables.

preparation time 10 minutes **cooking time** 10 minutes **serves** 4
nutritional count per serving 14.8g total fat (3.2g saturated fat);
1471kJ (352 cal); 6.2g carbohydrate; 45.6g protein; 5.6g fibre

Loin chops rogan josh with pulao salad

12 lamb loin chops (1.2kg)
½ cup (150g) rogan josh curry paste
1 ½ cups (300g) basmati rice
¼ teaspoon ground turmeric
1 cardamom pod, bruised
⅓ cup (45g) roasted slivered almonds
⅓ cup (55g) sultanas
⅓ cup firmly packed fresh coriander leaves
⅓ cup coarsely chopped fresh mint
mustard seed dressing
¼ cup (60ml) olive oil
2 tablespoons yellow mustard seeds
¼ cup (60ml) white wine vinegar
1 tablespoon white sugar

1 Combine lamb and paste in large bowl; turn lamb to coat in paste.
2 Make mustard seed dressing.
3 Cook rice, turmeric and cardamom in large saucepan of boiling water until rice is tender; drain.
4 Meanwhile, cook lamb, in batches, in heated oiled grill pan until cooked.
5 To make pulao salad, combine rice in large bowl with nuts, sultanas, herbs and dressing. Serve pulao salad with lamb.
mustard seed dressing Heat oil in small saucepan; cook seeds, stirring constantly, over low heat, until aromatic and softened. Place seeds, vinegar and sugar in screw-top jar; shake well.

preparation time 10 minutes **cooking time** 20 minutes **serves** 6
nutritional count per serving 41.6g total fat (11.6g saturated fat); 3072kJ (735 cal); 51.7g carbohydrate; 37.2g protein; 4.2g fibre

Souvlaki with tomato, almond and mint salad

¼ cup (60ml) olive oil
2 teaspoons finely grated lemon rind
¼ cup (60ml) lemon juice
¼ cup finely chopped fresh oregano
800g lamb fillets, cut into 3cm pieces
2 medium yellow capsicums (400g), chopped coarsely
1 medium red onion (150g), chopped coarsely
2 large tomatoes (440g), chopped coarsely
¼ cup (35g) roasted slivered almonds
1 cup firmly packed fresh mint leaves

1 Combine oil, rind, juice and oregano in screw-top jar; shake well.
2 Thread lamb, capsicum and onion, alternately, onto skewers. Place on baking tray; drizzle with half the dressing. Cook souvlaki on heated oiled grill plate (or grill or barbecue) until cooked as desired.
3 Meanwhile, combine tomato, nuts and mint with the remaining dressing in small bowl.
4 Serve souvlakia with tomato, almond and mint salad, and pitta bread, if desired.

preparation time 20 minutes **cooking time** 15 minutes **serves** 4
nutritional count per serving 26.1g total fat (5.5g saturated fat);
1914kJ (458 cal); 7.8g carbohydrate; 46.2g protein; 4.3g fibre
tip Soak 8 bamboo skewers in water for 30 minutes before using
to prevent scorching during cooking.

Sumac chicken with minted eggplant

1 teaspoon finely grated lemon rind
⅓ cup (80ml) lemon juice
2 teaspoons sumac
2 teaspoons caster sugar
1 tablespoon tahini
800g chicken tenderloins
2 medium eggplants (600g), sliced thickly
¼ cup (60ml) olive oil
½ cup coarsely chopped fresh mint
1 lemon (140g), sliced thickly

1 Combine rind, half the juice, sumac, sugar, tahini and chicken in large bowl.
2 Cook chicken on heated oiled grill plate (or grill or barbecue) until cooked through. Remove from heat; cover to keep warm.
3 Cook eggplant on cleaned heated oiled grill plate (or grill or barbecue) until browned; combine eggplant in medium bowl with remaining juice, oil and mint.
4 Serve chicken and eggplant with lemon.

preparation time 10 minutes **cooking time** 15 minutes **serves** 4
nutritional count per serving 28.3g total fat (5.7g saturated fat);
2107kJ (504 cal); 14.2g carbohydrate; 45.9g protein; 5.1g fibre
tip Tahini is a sesame seed paste available from Middle-Eastern food stores, many supermarkets and health-food stores.

glossary

allspice also known as pimento or jamaican pepper.

almonds

meal ground almonds.

slivered small pieces cut lengthways.

bacon rashers also called bacon slices.

basil, thai also called horapa; differs from holy basil and sweet basil in look and taste – smaller leaves, purplish stems and a slight aniseed taste.

beans

borlotti also called roman or pink beans; eaten fresh or dried. Interchangeable with pinto beans as they look similar – pale pink/beige with dark red streaks.

refried pinto or borlotti beans, cooked twice: first soaked and boiled, then mashed and fried. Available canned in supermarkets.

snake long (40cm), thin, round, fresh green beans; Asian in origin, similar in taste to green or french beans. Also called yard-long beans because of their (pre-metric) length.

white a generic term we use for canned or dried cannellini, haricot, navy or great northern beans which all belong to the *phaseolus vulgaris* family.

bicarbonate of soda also called baking soda.

broccolini a cross between broccoli and Chinese kale; long asparagus-like stems with a long loose floret, completely edible. Looks like broccoli but is milder and sweeter in taste.

buk choy also known as bok choy, pak choi, Chinese white cabbage or Chinese chard; has a fresh, mild mustard taste. Use stems and leaves. A commonly used Asian green.

butter we use salted butter unless stated otherwise.

buttermilk originally the term for the slightly sour liquid left after butter was churned from cream, today it is made like yogurt. Sold with milk products in supermarkets. Despite the implication, it is low in fat.

capers grey-green buds of a warm climate shrub, sold dried and salted or pickled in a vinegar brine; tiny young ones (baby capers) are available in brine or dried in salt.

capsicum also called pepper or bell pepper.

cardamom a spice native to India; can be purchased in pod, seed or ground form. Has a distinctive aromatic, sweetly rich flavour.

cheese

blue mould-treated cheeses mottled with blue veining. Varieties include firm and crumbly stilton types and mild, creamy brie-like cheeses.

bocconcini from the diminutive of "boccone", meaning mouthful in Italian; walnut-sized, baby mozzarella, a delicate, semi-soft, white cheese traditionally made from buffalo milk. Sold fresh, it spoils rapidly so will only keep, refrigerated in brine, for 1 or 2 days at the most.

fetta Greek in origin; a crumbly textured goat- or sheep-milk cheese having a sharp, salty taste. Ripened and stored in salted whey.

fontina an Italian cow-milk cheese that has a smooth but firm texture and a mild, nutty flavour. It is an ideal melting or grilling cheese. Use mozzarella or taleggio as a substitute.

haloumi a Greek Cypriot cheese having a semi-firm, spongy texture and salty yet sweet flavour. Ripened and stored in salted whey; it's best grilled or fried, and holds its shape well on being heated. Eat while warm as it becomes tough and rubbery on cooling.

jarlsberg brand-name of a popular Norwegian cheese made from cow milk; has large holes and a mild, nutty taste.

mascarpone an Italian fresh cultured-cream product made similarly to yogurt. Whiteish to creamy yellow in colour, with a buttery-rich, luscious texture. Soft, creamy and spreadable, it is used in desserts and as an accompaniment to a dessert of fresh fruit.

parmesan also called parmigiano; a hard, grainy cow-milk cheese originating in the Parma region of Italy. The curd is salted in brine for a month then aged for up to 2 years.

pizza cheese a commercial blend of varying proportions of grated mozzarella, cheddar and parmesan.

ricotta a soft, sweet, moist, white cow-milk cheese with a low fat content (8.5 per cent) and a slightly grainy texture. Its name roughly translates as "cooked again" and refers to ricotta's manufacture from a whey that is itself a by-product of other cheese making.

roquefort a blue cheese with a pungent taste; made only from the milk of specially bred sheep and ripened in the damp limestone caves found under the village of Roquefort-sur-Soulzon in France. Has a sticky, bone-coloured rind and, when ripe, the sharp, almost metallic-tasting interior is creamy and almost shiny.

chicken
breast fillets breast halved, skinned, boned.
thigh fillets thigh with skin and centre bone removed.

chickpeas also called garbanzos, hummus or channa; an irregularly round, sandy-coloured legume. Firm texture even after cooking, a floury mouth-feel and robust nutty flavour; available canned or dried (requires several hours soaking in cold water before use).

chilli
jalapeño pronounced hah-lah-pain-yo. Fairly hot, medium-sized, plump, dark green chilli; available pickled, sold canned or bottled, and fresh, from greengrocers.
thai also called "scuds"; tiny, very hot and bright red in colour.

chinese barbecued duck traditionally cooked in special ovens in China; dipped into and brushed during roasting with a coating of soy sauce, sherry, ginger, five-spice, star anise and hoisin sauce. Available from Asian food shops and Chinese barbecued meat shops.

chinese cooking wine also called hao hsing or chinese rice wine; made from fermented rice, wheat, sugar and salt with a 13.5 per cent alcohol content. Inexpensive and found in Asian food shops; if you can't find it, replace with mirin or sherry.

chocolate
dark eating also called semi-sweet or luxury chocolate; made of a high percentage of cocoa liquor and cocoa butter, and little added sugar. Unless stated otherwise, we use dark eating chocolate.

white eating contains no cocoa solids but derives its sweet flavour from cocoa butter. Very sensitive to heat.

chocolate hazelnut spread we use Nutella.

chorizo sausage of Spanish origin, made of coarsely ground pork and highly seasoned with garlic and chilli.

choy sum also called pakaukeo or flowering cabbage, a member of the buk choy family; has long stems, light green leaves and yellow flowers. Stems and leaves are both edible.

cinnamon available in pieces (sticks or quills) and ground; one of the most common spices.

cloves dried flower buds of a tropical tree; can be used whole or ground. Has a strong scent and taste; use sparingly.

coconut

cream obtained from the first pressing of coconut flesh, without added water. Available in cans and cartons at most supermarkets.

flaked dried flaked coconut flesh.

milk not the liquid inside but the diluted liquid from the second pressing. Available in cans and cartons at most supermarkets.

shredded unsweetened thin strips of dried coconut flesh.

coconut-flavoured liqueur we use Malibu.

coffee-flavoured liqueur we use either Kahlua or Tia Maria.

coppa is salted and dried pork neck or shoulder. Deep red in colour, found in both mild and spicy versions; it is more marbled with fat so it's less expensive.

cornflour also known as cornstarch.

cornichons French for gherkin, a very small variety of cucumber.

corn syrup a sweet syrup made by heating cornstarch with water under pressure. It comes in light and dark types; used in baking and confectionery. Available in some supermarkets, delicatessens and health food stores.

couscous a fine, grain-like cereal product; a semolina flour and water dough is sieved then dehydrated to produce minuscule even-sized pellets of couscous. Rehydrate by steaming or by adding warm liquid; it swells to three or four times its original size.

crème fraîche a mature, naturally fermented cream (minimum 35 per cent fat content) having a velvety texture and slightly tangy, nutty flavour. It can boil without curdling.

cumin also called zeera or comino; resembling caraway in size, cumin is the dried seed of a plant related to the parsley family. Has a spicy, curry-like flavour; found as seeds or ground.

daikon also called white radish; long, white horseradish has a sweet flavour. Peel before use, raw in salads or shredded as a garnish; also cooked in stir-fries. The flesh is white but the skin can be white or black; buy those that are firm and unwrinkled from Asian food shops.

dried cranberries have the same slightly sour, succulent flavour as fresh cranberries. Available in most supermarkets. Also available sweetened.

egg if a recipe calls for raw or barely cooked eggs, exercise caution if there is a salmonella problem in your area.

eggplant also known as aubergine.

fennel also called finocchio or anise. A crunchy green vegetable slightly resembling celery; eaten raw in salads, cooked or used as an ingredient.

five-spice powder usually contains ground cinnamon, cloves, star anise, sichuan pepper and fennel seeds. Available from most supermarkets or Asian food shops.

flour

besan also known as chickpea flour or gram; made from ground chickpeas so is gluten-free and high in protein.

plain also known as all-purpose flour.

rice very fine, almost powdery and gluten-free; ground white rice.

self-raising all-purpose flour with baking powder and salt; make at home in the proportion of 1 cup flour to 2 teaspoons baking powder.

wholemeal also called wholewheat; milled with the wheat germ making it higher in fibre and more nutritional than white flour.

garam masala literally means blended spices; contains cardamom, cinnamon, cloves, cumin, coriander and fennel, roasted then ground.

ginger

fresh also called green or root ginger; the thick gnarled root of a tropical plant. Store, peeled in a jar of dry sherry and refrigerated, or frozen in an airtight container.

ground also called powdered ginger; cannot be substituted for fresh.

pickled pink or red coloured and available from Asian food shops. Paper-thin shavings of ginger that are pickled in vinegar, sugar and natural colouring.

golden syrup a by-product of refined sugarcane; pure maple syrup or honey can be substituted.

hazelnuts also called filberts; plump, grape-size, rich, sweet nut with a brown inedible skin. Remove skin by rubbing heated nuts together vigorously in a tea-towel.

meal hazelnuts ground to a coarse flour texture.

kaffir lime leaves also called bai magrood and looks like two glossy dark green leaves joined end to end, forming a rounded hourglass shape. Sold fresh, dried or frozen, the dried leaves are less potent so double the number if using them as a substitute for fresh; a strip of fresh lime peel may be substituted for each kaffir lime leaf.

kecap asin a thick, dark, salty Indonesian soy sauce.

kecap manis dark, thick sweet soy sauce; the sweetness is derived from the addition of either molasses or palm sugar when brewed.

kumara the polynesian name of an orange-fleshed sweet potato often confused with yam.

lemon grass also known as takrai, serai or serah. A tall, clumping, lemon-smelling and tasting, sharp-edged aromatic tropical grass; the white lower part of the stem is used, finely chopped. Can be found, fresh, dried, powdered and frozen, in supermarkets and Asian food shops.

macadamias native to Australia; fairly large, slightly soft, buttery rich nut. Refrigerate nuts to prevent rancidity due to their high oil content.

maple syrup distilled from the sap of sugar maple trees found only in Canada and some states in the USA. Maple-flavoured syrup is not an adequate substitute.

milk we use full-cream homogenised milk unless stated otherwise.

miso fermented soy bean paste. Buy in tubs or plastic packs.

mizuna Japanese in origin; the frizzy green salad leaves have a delicate mustard flavour.

mushrooms

button small, cultivated white mushrooms with a mild flavour; use when a recipe calls for an unspecified mushroom.

oyster also known as abalone; grey-white and shaped like a fan, with a smooth texture and subtle, oyster-like flavour.

shiitake fresh, are also known as Chinese black, forest or golden oak mushrooms. Although cultivated, they have the earthiness and taste of wild mushrooms. They are large and meaty.

swiss brown also called roman or cremini. Light to dark brown in colour with full-bodied flavour.

mustard

dijon also called french. Pale brown, creamy, distinctively flavoured, mild French mustard.

wholegrain also called seeded. A French-style coarse-grain mustard made from crushed mustard seeds and dijon-style french mustard.

noodles

hokkien also called stir-fry noodles; fresh wheat noodles look like thick, yellow-brown spaghetti and need no pre-cooking before use.

rice stick also called sen lek or kway teow. They come in different widths, soak all in hot water to soften.

rice vermicelli also called sen mee or mei fun. Used in spring rolls and cold salads. Before use, soak dried noodles in hot water until soft, boil briefly then rinse with hot water.

soba thin, pale-brown Japanese noodle; made from buckwheat and wheat flour. Available dried and fresh, and in flavoured varieties.

nutmeg a strong and pungent spice ground from the dried nut of an Indonesian evergreen tree. Usually bought ground, the flavour is more intense if freshly ground from the whole nut (buy in spice shops).

oil

cooking spray we use a cholesterol-free spray made from canola oil.

olive made from ripened olives. Extra virgin and virgin are the first and second press, respectively, of the olives and are considered the best; types named "extra light" or "light" refer to taste not fat levels.

peanut pressed from ground peanuts; the most commonly used oil in Asian cooking due to its capacity to handle high heat without burning.

sesame made from roasted, crushed, white sesame seeds; used as a flavouring rather than a cooking medium.

onion

fried onion/shallots used as a condiment; available in cellophane bags or jars at Asian food shops; if tightly sealed, they will keep for months.

green also known as scallion or (incorrectly) shallot; an immature onion picked before the bulb has formed, has a long, bright-green stalk.

purple shallots also called Asian shallots; related to the onion but looks like garlic (in tight clusters). Thin layered and intensely flavoured.

shallots also called French shallots, golden shallots or eschalots; small, elongated, brown-skinned members of the onion family. Grows in tight clusters like garlic.

pancetta an Italian unsmoked bacon, pork belly cured in salt and spices then rolled and dried for weeks. Used as an ingredient rather than eaten on its own.

pepitas pale green kernels of dried pumpkin seeds; plain or salted.

pine nuts also known as pignoli; not a nut but a small, cream-coloured kernel from pine cones. They are best roasted before use.

polenta also cornmeal; a flour-like cereal made of dried corn (maize). Also the name of the dish made from it.

preserved lemon whole or quartered salted lemons preserved in olive oil and lemon juice. Available from delicatessens and specialty food shops. Use the rind only and rinse well under cold water before using.

prosciutto unsmoked Italian ham; salted, air-cured and aged, it is usually eaten uncooked.

rhubarb classified as a vegetable, is eaten as a fruit and therefore considered one. Leaves must be removed before cooking as they can contain traces of poison; the edible crisp, pink-red stalks are cooked.

rice

arborio small, round grain well-suited to absorb large amounts of liquid; ideal for risotto.

basmati a white, fragrant long-grained rice; the grains fluff up beautifully when cooked. Wash several times before cooking.

jasmine a long-grained perfumed white rice; moist in texture, it clings together after cooking.

rocket also known as arugula, rugula and rucola; peppery green leaf eaten raw in salads or used in cooking.

sambal oelek also ulek or olek; a salty Indonesian paste of ground chillies and vinegar.

sauces

char siu also called Chinese barbecue sauce; a paste-like ingredient dark-red-brown with a sharp sweet and spicy flavour. Made with fermented soy beans, honey and spices.

fish called naam pla (Thai) and nuoc naam (Vietnamese). Made from pulverised salted fermented fish; has a pungent smell and strong taste, use according to taste.

oyster thick, rich brown sauce made from oysters and their brine, cooked with salt and soy sauce, thickened with starches.

soy also called sieu. Made from fermented soybeans, several variations are available in Asian food stores and supermarkets; we use Japanese soy sauce.

sesame seeds black and white are the most common of this small oval seed. Toast the seeds in a heavy-based frying pan over low heat.

sichuan peppercorns also called szechuan pepper. A mildly hot spice from the prickly ash tree.

silver beet also called Swiss chard or, incorrectly, spinach; has fleshy stalks and large leaves.

sopressa a semi-hard pork salami flavoured with pepper, cinnamon, cloves, nutmeg, garlic and rosemary; has a delicate, sweet taste.

spinach also called english spinach and incorrectly, silver beet.

sugar

brown a very soft, fine granulated sugar retaining molasses for colour and flavour.

caster also called superfine or finely granulated table sugar; dissolves easily.

icing also known as confectioners' sugar; pulverised granulated sugar crushed with a little cornflour.

palm also known as nam tan pip, jaggery or jawa; made from the sap of the sugar palm tree. Light brown or black, often sold in rock-hard cakes; use brown sugar if unavailable.

sumac a purple-red, astringent spice ground from berries of a wild Mediterranean shrub; adds a tart, lemony flavour. Available in Middle Eastern food stores.

tamarind the tamarind tree produces clusters of hairy brown pods, each filled with seeds and a viscous pulp, that are dried and pressed into blocks of tamarind found in Asian food shops. Gives a sweet-sour, astringent taste.

turmeric also called kamin; a rhizome related to ginger and galangal. Must be pounded or grated to release its acrid aroma and pungent flavour. Fresh turmeric can be substituted with the more common powder.

vanilla bean dried, long, thin pod; the minuscule black seeds inside are used to impart a luscious vanilla flavour.

vinegar

balsamic originally from Modena, Italy, there are now many on the market. Quality can be determined up to a point by price; use the most expensive sparingly.

rice a colourless vinegar made from fermented rice, flavoured with sugar and salt.

wasabi also called wasabe; an Asian horseradish used to make the pungent, green-coloured sauce traditionally served with Japanese raw fish dishes; sold in powdered or paste form.

wombok also called Chinese cabbage, peking or napa cabbage; elongated in shape with pale green, crinkly leaves.

yogurt we use plain full-cream yogurt unless stated otherwise.

zucchini also known as courgette.

index

A

aïoli 45
  buttermilk 301
  coriander 50
almonds
  almond and berry
    smoothie 121
  almond and coriander
    chicken with lemon
    mayonnaise 176
  coffee almond
    biscuits 150
  pear and almond
    friands 162
  pear, chocolate and
    almond galette 318
  sichuan eggplant,
    almond and wombok
    stir-fry 310
  souvlaki with tomato,
    almond and mint
    salad 382
apples
  apple, pear and
    ginger juice 13
  apple salsa 273
  apples, caramelised
    228
asian greens, steamed,
  with char siu sauce
  302
asian-style fried egg
  with mushrooms 191

B

bacon
  bacon and corn
    pizza 129
  blueberry buttermilk
    pancakes with
    bacon 22
  potato and bacon
    pizza 65
balsamic rosemary
  grilled veal steaks 377
balsamic strawberries
  with mascarpone 317

banana
  banana caramel
    sundae 236
  banana, date and rolled
    oat cookies 142
  butterscotch nougat
    bananas 232
  passionfruit and
    banana sundae 330
  ricotta and banana
    toasts 26
basil mayonnaise 274
béchamel, cheese 74
beef
  beef burgers 62
  beef kway teow 207
  char-grilled steak and
    vegetables with baba
    ghanoush 354
  chilli-garlic mince with
    snake beans 254
  grilled steak and
    vegie-salsa
    sandwich 73
  herbed rib-eye with
    tapenade mash 362
  hokkien chilli beef 203
  orange, beetroot and
    roast beef salad 78
  peppered fillet steaks
    with creamy bourbon
    sauce 270
berries
  berry, coconut and
    yogurt parfaits 329
  berry hazelnut
    crumbles 239
  berry yogurt muffins
    137
bhaji, spicy carrot and
  zucchini 309
biscuits/cookies
  banana, date and rolled
    oat cookies 142
  brown sugar and
    pecan biscuits 149

(*biscuits/cookies*
  continued)
  chocolate chip
    cookies 161
  coffee almond
    biscuits 150
  cranberry and
    coconut biscuits 145
  golden pecan
    twists 157
  maple-syrup butter
    cookies 154
  polenta and orange
    biscuits 141
  vanilla bean thins 165
  white chocolate
    macadamia cookies
    134
black olive tapenade
  245
blt on croissant 45
blueberry buttermilk
  pancakes with
  bacon 22
brandy snap and
  rhubarb stacks 325
brown sugar and pecan
  biscuits 149
bruschetta fingers 118
burgers
  beef 62
  spiced lamb burger
    with tzatziki 365
  thai fish 345
buttermilk
  aïoli 301
  dressing 269
  buttermilk fruit
    smoothie 113
  butterscotch nougat
    bananas 232

C

caesar dressing 278,
  294
caesar-style potato
  salad 294

392

capers and anchovies, pasta with 175
caramel sauce 236, 334
char sui pork, corn and choy sum 220
cheese
béchamel 74
cheesy scrambled eggs with spinach 18
cheesy-vegie pasta bake 195
cherry tomatoes, roasted, fetta, avocado and basil 37
chicken, tomato and fetta patties with spinach salad 171
coppa and ricotta panini 94
corn and goat cheese quesadillas 70
corn, cheese and carrot omelettes 34
fetta and artichoke pizzetta 69
ham, egg and cheese toastie 106
ham, sage and fontina pizza 86
honeyed ricotta and pears 17
italian egg, prosciutto and cheese roll 10
lamb, bocconcini and gremolata stacks 289
lemon, pea and ricotta pasta 224
pumpkin and fetta pizza 122
ricotta and banana toasts 26
smoked cheese and sopressa pizza 102
warm pasta, pea and ricotta salad 301

cherry tomatoes, roasted, fetta, avocado and basil 37
chicken
almond and coriander chicken with lemon mayonnaise 176
chicken and yellow bean relish 204
chicken, lentil and cauliflower pilaf 168
chicken margherita 286
chicken quesadilla 126
chicken sang choy bow 187
chicken, tomato and fetta patties with spinach salad 171
chicken yakitori with sesame dipping sauce 350
chilli fried rice with chicken and broccolini 196
cranberry and pine nut pilaf with chicken 293
ginger-plum chicken and noodle stir-fry 216
italian chicken patties on focaccia 77
pesto chicken with grilled zucchini 370
piri piri chicken thigh fillets 349
sake chicken 297
smoked chicken, radicchio and basil leaf salad 58
sumac chicken with minted eggplant 385
turkish chicken club sandwich 50

chilli
chilli fried rice with chicken and broccolini 196
chilli-garlic mince with snake beans 254
chilli lime dressing 285
chilli squid salad 249
chocolate see also white chocolate
choc-malt smoothie 117
chocolate chip cookies 161
pear, chocolate and almond galette 318
pears with choc-mint sauce 231
chorizo and white bean braise 188
citrus salad with lime and mint granita 322
coconut-poached fish with spinach 313
coffee almond biscuits 150
cookies see biscuits/ cookies
coppa and ricotta panini 94
coriander aïoli 50
corn and goat cheese quesadillas 70
corn, cheese and carrot omelettes 34
couscous, carrot and pistachio pilaf 262
crab and soba salad with ginger miso dressing 282
cranberry and coconut biscuits 145
cranberry and pine nut pilaf with chicken 293
croque madame 74

D

desserts
balsamic strawberries
with mascarpone 317
banana caramel
sundae 236
berry, coconut and
yogurt parfaits 329
berry hazelnut
crumbles 239
brandy snap and
rhubarb stacks 325
butterscotch nougat
bananas 232
citrus salad with
lime and mint
granita 322
hazelnut tiramisu 326
lemon and mixed
berry self-saucing
pudding 235
mango galettes with
coconut cream 333
passionfruit and
banana sundae 330
passionfruit soufflés
314
pavlova trifle 321
pear, chocolate and
almond galette 318
pears with choc-mint
sauce 231
rice pudding with
cardamom and
raisins 228
walnut and ricotta-
stuffed figs 334
dips
moroccan carrot 266
white bean 277
dressings 306
buttermilk 269
caesar 278, 294
chilli lime 285
ginger miso 282
lemon anchovy 172

(*dressings* continued)
lime 265
lime and palm
sugar 305
mustard seed 381
pesto 58
sumac 262
drinks *see also* juices;
smoothies
hot mocha 29
indian chai 41
duck, vietnamese
salad 265

E

eggplant, roasted, and
chorizo pizza 54
eggs
asian-style fried egg
with mushrooms 191
cheesy scrambled
eggs with spinach 18
corn, cheese and
carrot omelettes 34
croque madame 74
egg drop soup 57
ham, egg and cheese
toastie 106
herb omelette with
sautéed mushrooms
14
huevos rancheros 38
italian egg, prosciutto
and cheese roll 10
spinach, ham and
poached egg 30

F

fattoush 369
felafel 97
fetta and artichoke
pizzetta 69
fish *see also* seafood
coconut-poached fish
with spinach 313
grilled salmon with
nam jim and herb
salad 357

(*fish* continued)
lemon grass fish with
daikon salad 258
lemon salmon patties
on turkish bread 89
lime and chilli roasted
snapper 285
orange and soy
salmon parcels 378
pan-fried fish with
fennel salad 250
teriyaki salmon with
soba salad 373
thai fish burgers 345
tuna and chilli
pasta 199
frappé
kiwifruit and mint 125
pineapple and
rockmelon 21
friands
lemon and coconut 146
pear and almond 162

G

ginger miso dressing
282
ginger-plum chicken
and noodle stir-fry 216
golden pecan twists 157
greek salad with grilled
lamb 338
green olive salsa 353
gremolata 289

H

ham, egg and cheese
toastie 106
ham, sage and fontina
pizza 86
hazelnut tiramisu 326
herb omelette with
sautéed mushrooms 14
herb salad 357
herbed-crumbed lamb
racks 257
herbed beef rib-eye with
tapenade mash 362

hoisin dipping sauce 281
hokkien chilli beef 203
honeyed ricotta and pears 17
huevos rancheros 38

I
indian chai 41
italian chicken patties on focaccia 77
italian egg, prosciutto and cheese roll 10

J
javanese stir-fried pork and rice noodles 227
juices
  apple, pear and ginger 13
  peach and raspberry 46

K
kaffir lime and rice salad with tofu and cashews 305
kebabs, pork fillet and pancetta 366
kipflers, barbecued 353
kiwifruit and mint frappé 125
kumara, rosemary and caramelised onion pizza 81
kway teow, beef 207

L
lamb
  greek salad with grilled lamb 338
  herbed-crumbed lamb racks 257
  lamb, bocconcini and gremolata stacks 289
  lamb cutlets niçoise 172
  lamb loin chops rogan josh with pulao salad 381

(*lamb* continued)
  lamb racks with mustard maple glaze 298
  lamb teriyaki with broccolini 179
  minty lamb cutlets with mixed vegie smash 342
  pitta filled with lamb and tabbouleh 101
  souvlaki with tomato, almond and mint salad 382
  spiced lamb burger with tzatziki 365
  tandoori lamb cutlets with fresh melon and coconut chutney 341
  turkish lamb and yogurt salad 66
lemon grass fish with daikon salad 258
lemons
  lemon anchovy dressing 172
  lemon and coconut friands 146
  lemon and mixed berry self-saucing pudding 235
  lemon mayonnaise 176
  lemon, pea and ricotta pasta 224
  lemon salmon patties on turkish bread 89
lentils, red curry 223
limes
  lime and chilli roasted snapper 285
  lime and palm sugar dressing 305
  lime dressing 265

M
mango galettes with coconut cream 333
maple-syrup butter cookies 154
mayonnaise
  basil 274
  lemon 176
mexican pork cutlets with avocado salsa 358
minty lamb cutlets with mixed vegie smash 342
mixed berry smoothie 25
mixed vegie smash 342
mocha, hot 29
moroccan carrot dip 266
moroccan pizzetta 85
muffins
  berry yogurt 137
  yogurt, berry and white chocolate 153
mushrooms
  asian-style fried egg with mushrooms 191
  mixed mushroom stroganoff 183
mussels in black bean sauce 253
mustard maple glaze 298
mustard seed dressing 381

N
nam jim 357
noodles
  crab and soba salad with ginger miso dressing 282

(*noodles* continued)
ginger-plum chicken
and noodle
stir-fry 216
javanese stir-fried pork
and rice noodles 227
pad thai 212

O
orange and soy salmon
parcels 378
orange, beetroot and
roast beef salad 78

P
pad thai 212
pancakes
blueberry buttermilk,
with bacon 22
pancetta and radicchio
rigatoni 261
passionfruit and banana
sundae 330
passionfruit soufflés
314
pasta
capers and anchovies,
with 175
cheesy-vegie pasta
bake 195
lemon, pea and
ricotta 224
pancetta and radicchio
rigatoni 261
pumpkin and sage
ravioli 200
ravioli with tomato,
pea and basil sauce
211
spaghetti carbonara
with peas 208
tuna and chilli pasta
199
warm pasta, pea and
ricotta 301
pavlova trifle 321
peach and raspberry
juice 46

pears
pear and almond
friands 162
pear and roquefort
salad 269
pear, chocolate and
almond galette 318
pears with choc-mint
sauce 231
peppered fillet steaks
with creamy bourbon
sauce 270
pepperoni pizzetta 61
pesto chicken with
grilled zucchini 370
pesto dressing 58
pesto, ham and
mushroom pizza 114
pineapple and
rockmelon frappé 21
piri piri chicken thigh
fillets 349
pitta filled with lamb
and tabbouleh 101
pizza
bacon and corn 129
ham, sage and
fontina 86
kumara, rosemary and
caramelised onion 81
pesto, ham and
mushroom 114
pizza mexicana 110
potato and bacon 65
pumpkin and fetta 122
roasted eggplant and
chorizo 54
smoked cheese and
sopressa 102
pizzetta
fetta and artichoke 69
moroccan 85
pepperoni 61
pizzetta caprese 98
polenta and orange
biscuits 141

pork
char sui pork, corn
and choy sum 220
grilled pork loin chops
with apple and onion
plum sauce 374
javanese stir-fried
pork and rice
noodles 227
mexican pork cutlets
with avocado salsa
358
pad thai 212
pork fillet and pancetta
kebabs 366
pork fried rice 215
pork, kumara mash
and apple salsa 273
pork larb with
broccolini 184
porridge with honeyed
coconut and dried
fruit 42
potato and bacon
pizza 65
prawns
seafood in lemon
cream sauce 346
vietnamese prawn
rolls 281
pumpkin and chickpea
ratatouille 180
pumpkin and fetta
pizza 122
pumpkin and sage
ravioli 200

Q
quesadillas
chicken 126
corn and goat
cheese 70

R
radicchio parcels,
char-grilled 361
radicchio, pumpkin and
haloumi salad 306

ratatouille, pumpkin and
  chickpea 180
ravioli
  pumpkin and sage 200
  tomato, pea and basil
  sauce, with 211
red curry lentils 223
red wine vinaigrette 90
relish, chicken and
  yellow bean 204
rice
  chicken, lentil and
  cauliflower pilaf 168
  chilli fried rice with
  chicken and
  broccolini 196
  couscous, carrot and
  pistachio pilaf 262
  cranberry and pine
  nut pilaf with
  chicken 293
  kaffir lime and rice
  salad with tofu and
  cashews 305
  pork fried rice 215
  rice pudding with
  cardamom and
  raisins 228
ricotta and banana
  toasts 26
rigatoni
  pancetta and
  radicchio 261

S
sake chicken 297
salads
  caesar salad with salt
  and pepper squid 278
  caesar-style potato
  salad 294
  chilli squid 249
  crab and soba salad
  with ginger miso
  dressing 282
  greek salad with
  grilled lamb 338

(*salads* continued)
  herb 357
  kaffir lime and rice
  salad with tofu and
  cashews 305
  orange, beetroot and
  roast beef 78
  pear and roquefort
  269
  radicchio, pumpkin and
  haloumi salad 306
  salami, bocconcini
  and pasta 90
  turkish lamb and
  yogurt 66
  vietnamese duck
  salad 265
  warm pasta, pea and
  ricotta 301
  zucchini and sumac
  fritters with tomato
  and mint salad 246
salami, bocconcini and
  pasta salad 90
salsa verde 290
sang choy bow,
  chicken 187
sauces
  caramel 236, 334
  hoisin dipping 281
  mixed berry 235
  sesame dipping 350
  tomato 10
  yogurt 97
scones with strawberries
  and cream 138
seafood *see also* fish
  caesar salad with
  salt and pepper
  squid 278
  chilli, salt and pepper
  242
  chilli squid salad 249
  crab and soba salad
  with ginger miso
  dressing 282

(*seafood* continued)
  lemon cream sauce,
  in 346
  mussels in black bean
  sauce 253
  pad thai 212
  vietnamese prawn
  rolls 281
sichuan eggplant,
  almond and wombok
  stir-fry 310
smoothies
  almond and berry 121
  buttermilk fruit 113
  choc-malt 117
  mixed berry 25
  strawberry soy 109
soufflé, passionfruit 314
soups
  egg drop 57
  soup with pistou 53
souvlaki with tomato,
  almond and mint salad
  382
spaghetti carbonara
  with peas 208
spicy carrot and zucchini
  bhaji 309
spicy veal pizzaiola 219
spinach and beetroot
  tart 93
spinach, ham and
  poached egg 30
squid
  caesar salad with salt
  and pepper squid 278
  chilli squid salad 249
stir-fries
  ginger-plum chicken
  and noodle 216
  javanese stir-fried
  pork and rice
  noodles 227
  sichuan eggplant,
  almond and
  wombok 310

(*stir-fries* continued)
tofu, cashew and
vegie 192
strawberries
balsamic strawberries
with mascarpone
317
strawberries and
cream on brioche 33
strawberry soy
smoothie 109
stroganoff, mixed
mushroom 183
sumac chicken with
minted eggplant
385
sumac dressing 262

T
tandoori lamb cutlets
with fresh melon
and coconut chutney
341
tapenade, black olive
245
tarts
spinach and
beetroot 93
sticky pecan 158
tomato, pesto and
olive 82
teriyaki salmon with
soba salad 373
thai fish burgers 345
tofu, cashew and
vegie stir-fry 192
tomatoes
chicken, tomato and
fetta patties with
spinach salad 171
fresh tomato salsa 38
roasted cherry
tomatoes, fetta,
avocado and basil 37
sauce 10
tomato, pesto and
olive tart 82

tuna and chilli pasta
199
turkey on toasted
turkish bread 130
turkish chicken club
sandwich 50
turkish lamb and
yogurt salad 66

V
vanilla bean thins 165
veal
balsamic rosemary
grilled veal steaks
377
spicy veal pizzaiola
219
veal and asparagus
with basil mayonnaise
274
veal cutlets with
green olive salsa
353
veal scaloppine with
salsa verde 290
za'atar-spiced veal
loin chops with
fattoush 369
vietnamese duck
salad 265
vietnamese prawn
rolls 281
vinaigrette
red wine 90

W
walnut and ricotta-
stuffed figs 334
white bean dip 277
white chocolate *see
also* chocolate
white chocolate
macadamia
cookies 134
yogurt, berry and
white chocolate
muffins 153

Y
yogurt
sauce 97
yogurt, berry and
white chocolate
muffins 153

Z
za'atar 369
za'atar-spiced veal
loin chops with
fattoush 369
zucchini and sumac
fritters with tomato
and mint salad 246

conversion chart

MEASURES

One Australian metric measuring cup holds approximately 250ml, one Australian metric tablespoon holds 20ml, one Australian metric teaspoon holds 5ml.

The difference between one country's measuring cups and another's is within a two- or three-teaspoon variance, and will not affect your cooking results.North America, New Zealand and the United Kingdom use a 15ml tablespoon.

All cup and spoon measurements are level. The most accurate way of measuring dry ingredients is to weigh them. When measuring liquids, use a clear glass or plastic jug with the metric markings.

We use large eggs with an average weight of 60g.

LIQUID MEASURES

METRIC	IMPERIAL
30ml	1 fluid oz
60ml	2 fluid oz
100ml	3 fluid oz
125ml	4 fluid oz
150ml	5 fluid oz (¼ pint/1 gill)
190ml	6 fluid oz
250ml	8 fluid oz
300ml	10 fluid oz (½ pint)
500ml	16 fluid oz
600ml	20 fluid oz (1 pint)
1000ml (1 litre)	1¾ pints

LENGTH MEASURES

METRIC	IMPERIAL
3mm	⅛in
6mm	¼in
1cm	½in
2cm	¾in
2.5cm	1in
5cm	2in
6cm	2½in
8cm	3in
10cm	4in
13cm	5in
15cm	6in
18cm	7in
20cm	8in
23cm	9in
25cm	10in
28cm	11in
30cm	12in (1ft)

DRY MEASURES

METRIC	IMPERIAL
15g	½oz
30g	1oz
60g	2oz
90g	3oz
125g	4oz (¼lb)
155g	5oz
185g	6oz
220g	7oz
250g	8oz (½lb)
280g	9oz
315g	10oz
345g	11oz
375g	12oz (¾lb)
410g	13oz
440g	14oz
470g	15oz
500g	16oz (1lb)
750g	24oz (1½lb)
1kg	32oz (2lb)

OVEN TEMPERATURES

These oven temperatures are only a guide for conventional ovens.
For fan-forced ovens, check the manufacturer's manual.

	°C (CELSIUS)	°F (FAHRENHEIT)	GAS MARK
Very slow	120	250	½
Slow	150	275 – 300	1 – 2
Moderately slow	160	325	3
Moderate	180	350 – 375	4 – 5
Moderately hot	200	400	6
Hot	220	425 – 450	7 – 8
Very hot	240	475	9

General manager Christine Whiston
Editorial director Susan Tomnay
Creative director Hieu Chi Nguyen
Art director Caryl Wiggins
Senior editors Stephanie Kistner, Wendy Bryant
Food director Pamela Clark
Test Kitchen manager + nutritional information Belinda Farlow
Recipe consultant Louise Patniotis
Director of sales Brian Cearnes
Marketing manager Bridget Cody
Senior business analyst Rebecca Varela
Operations manager David Scotto
Production manager Victoria Jefferys
International rights enquiries Laura Bamford
lbamford@acpuk.com

ACP Books are published by ACP Magazines
a division of PBL Media Pty Limited
Publishing director, Women's lifestyle Pat Ingram
Director of sales, Women's lifestyle Lynette Phillips
Commercial manager, Women's lifestyle Seymour Cohen
Marketing director, Women's lifestyle Matthew Dominello
Public relations manager, Women's lifestyle Hannah Deveraux
Research director, Women's lifestyle Justin Stone
PBL Media, Chief Executive Officer Ian Law

Produced by ACP Books, Sydney.
Published by ACP Books, a division of ACP Magazines Ltd.
54 Park St, Sydney NSW Australia 2000. GPO Box 4088, Sydney, NSW 2001.
Phone +61 2 9282 8618 Fax +61 2 9267 9438
acpbooks@acpmagazines.com.au www.acpbooks.com.au
Printed by Toppan Printing Co., China.

Australia Distributed by Network Services, GPO Box 4088, Sydney, NSW 2001.
Phone +61 2 9282 8777 Fax +61 2 9264 3278 networkweb@networkservicescompany.com.au
United Kingdom Distributed by Australian Consolidated Press (UK),
10 Scirocco Close, Moulton Park Office Village, Northampton, NN3 6AP.
Phone +44 1604 642 200 Fax +44 1604 642 300
books@acpuk.com www.acpuk.com
New Zealand Distributed by Southern Publishers Group, 21 Newton Road, Auckland.
Phone +64 9 360 0692 Fax +64 9 360 0695 hub@spg.co.nz
South Africa Distributed by PSD Promotions, 30 Diesel Road Isando, Gauteng Johannesburg.
PO Box 1175, Isando 1600, Gauteng Johannesburg.
Phone +27 11 392 6065/6/7 Fax +27 11 392 6079/80 orders@psdprom.co.za
Canada Distributed by Publishers Group Canada
Order Desk & Customer Service 9050 Shaughnessy Street, Vancouver BC V6P 6E5
Phone (800) 663 5714 Fax (800) 565 3770 service@raincoast.com

Title: Fast: Australian women's weekly/food director Pamela Clark
ISBN: 978-1-86396-870-6 (pbk)
Notes: Includes index
Subjects: Quick and easy cookery
Other authors/contributors: Clark, Pamela
Also titled: Australian women's weekly
Dewey number: 641.555
© ACP Magazines Ltd 2009
ABN 18 053 273 546

To order books, phone 136 116 (within Australia).
Send recipe enquiries to: recipeenquiries@acpmagazines.com.au

Front cover Kumara, rosemary and caramelised onion pizza, page 81
Front cover photographer Ben Dearnley
Front cover stylist Vanessa Austin
Front cover photochef Belinda Farlow
Illustrations Hannah Blackmore
Back cover photographer Brett Stevens
Back cover stylist David Morgan